CARAVANNING

BARRY WILLIAMS

Illustrated by
Tri-Art

TVTimes FAMILY BOOKS

INDEPENDENT TELEVISION BOOKS LTD, LONDON

INDEPENDENT TELEVISION BOOKS LTD
247 Tottenham Court Road
London W1P 0AU

© Barry Williams 1975

ISBN 0 900 72734 9

Printed in Great Britain by
Butler and Tanner Ltd
Frome and London

Also avilable in this series:

BEATING THE COST OF COOKING
Mary Berry

DEAR KATIE
Katie Boyle

HOUSE PLANTS MADE EASY
Jean Taylor

KNOW YOUR CAR
John Dyson

KNOW YOUR RIGHTS
Dr Michael Winstanley and
Ruth Dunkley

POWER TOOLS AT HOME
Harold King

CONTENTS

Chapter 1
Why caravanning?

The fact that you have chosen to read this book, or part of it, means that you already have some interest in caravanning. Probably you know someone with a trailer caravan or a permanently sited holiday home by the sea, or perhaps you have seen friends or neighbours—maybe even total strangers—setting off with a van hitched to the back of their car and the

Caravan holidays bring freedom—to go where you please when you please. Modern tourers are easy to tow provided you follow a few simple rules when choosing a model to match your tow car

idea has struck you that caravanning could provide an answer to your family's holiday needs.

There's a good chance that it could. About one person in every six in Britain today enjoys a caravan holiday at some time in the year, so you can see it's already a pretty popular pastime. This figure includes those who stay in 'holiday homes', which is the correct term for caravans that are more or less static (though they can be moved as they are), and those that use touring trailer caravans, which are generally referred to simply as 'tourers' or 'trailer vans'. This book is written for those of you who are interested in the second type, though a great deal of the information will apply to holidaying in both types of van.

If you are thinking of making a start in caravanning, you'll have a lot of questions at the back of your mind. How difficult is it to tow a trailer? Do caravans cost a lot? How much wear will it cause my car? And are all those stories of jammed roads and wives complaining that it's no holiday for them really true? Don't worry, we've all had the same feeling . . . and most of us have come to the conclusion that caravanning is the ideal way to take a relaxed, do-as-you-please holiday.

One of the first aims of this book is to help you avoid the pitfalls that might otherwise make you give up caravanning without giving it a fair trial. The other important thing to remember is that you are new to the game. There are lots of caravanners around and you'll find that the great majority are only too pleased to give advice about all aspects of their hobby. In particular, you'll find a great sense of camaraderie at the caravan site, where most owners are delighted to show you their caravans and the modifications they have made to make life on the road and on the site more comfortable and enjoyable.

First, then, to the point uppermost in many people's minds: is caravanning expensive? Answering this is like trying to answer the old chestnut: 'How long is a piece of string?', because there is virtually no end to what you can spend on your towing car and trailer. But to put it into perspective, caravanning is not expensive when you consider that buying and maintaining a *new* caravan should cost you no more than holidaying at a hotel or guest house with your family over three or four years—and your caravan should last considerably longer than that! Added to this of course is the advantage that during those three or four years you will have limitless opportunities for second holidays and long weekends away from home at little or no extra cost. Sometimes you can find bargains in second-hand caravans; they are in short supply, but there is little that can go wrong with vans only a few years old.

You might even think of recouping some of your initial cost later by renting out your caravan to friends for their holidays—but more of this later. Once you have bought your van and a few basic essentials and your

car is suitably equipped for towing, you and your family can set off down the holiday road at almost a moment's notice. You'll find the overnight fees at most caravan sites extremely reasonable, and your only other running costs once you are on site are for gas (for cooking and maybe lighting) and the food you eat.

You will soon find that caravanning not only brings all the natural advantages of a holiday in the open air but will open up new friendships. How often have you stayed at a strange hotel, knowing no one and wondering what on earth to do during that spare hour or two before dinner? To campers and caravanners the site is their hotel, but because they are brought together by a common interest, many of the usual barriers are broken down.

There are caravan dealers spread all over the country, some specializing in particular makes and some with a very varied selection of makes and types. Most reputable traders are members of the National Caravan Council, the industry's trade organization

Caravanning has a special appeal for families with young children. It's the ideal way to introduce young people to the countryside and the excitement of foreign touring, and parents have none of the worries, complications or expense associated with more formal hotel accommodation

On the other hand, don't run off with the idea that wherever you go you'll be expected to join in holiday-camp-type games or invite the neighbours in to reminisce on last year's trip to the Continent; there are plenty of secluded sites where just you and the family can be together.

Caravanning will broaden your interests as well as your circle of friends, and countless numbers of caravanners have developed interests in subjects like photography, nature study, geology and bird-watching – hobbies for which the caravan provides the ideal mobile base, as you are not tied to it for mealtimes or venues. And if you are keen on football, horse-racing or whatever, you can take your caravan to matches or meetings away from home when you wouldn't be able to afford more conventional accommodation.

For children – as well as their parents – caravanning offers the ideal way to see places and enjoy new experiences; to visit foreign countries (there is nothing quite like touring abroad with a trailer for getting to know the people of other lands as they really are) as well as far-away areas of Britain

For people interested in a particular hobby or sport the touring caravan offers the ideal answer to the problems of finding on-the-spot accommodation. This site near Louth, Lincolnshire, has a well-stocked lake for fishermen, boating, swimming pool, licensed club, shops, a cinema and a café

without all the expense of more formal accommodation. Whatever the age of the family, Mum can prepare meals she knows everyone likes and they can sit down to eat when and where they please.

A big plus—when you are on the road you can pull in to the side for a quick 'brew-up', a much-needed wash and change or even an hour or so's sleep at any time. But do make sure you get right off the road, and don't be tempted to spend the whole night there. There's nothing worse than being woken up at three o'clock in the morning by a policeman who says you are causing an obstruction....

Caravan outfits aren't the easiest of things for other road-users to overtake, but a well-matched car and trailer in the right hands can be pretty nimble. British caravanners have recently been relieved of the burden of the 40 mph speed limit (for most outfits—in fact for all those with a sensible car-to-caravan weight ratio—the limit is now 50 mph) and this has gone some way to overcome the image of the trailer caravan as a mobile road-block.

Provided your car and caravan outfit conforms with a few basic legal requirements (see Chapter 7), you will be allowed to travel at speeds up to 50 mph on British roads not subject to a lower limit. Cars drawing trailers, however, are banned from the outside lane of three-lane motorways

Many old hands at caravanning in Britain may tell you that there are more restrictions these days than ever before: the idea has become so popular that sites get fully booked—and having to reserve your pitch at the site in advance has taken some of the fun out of caravanning. To a limited extent this is true I suppose, and over a Bank Holiday weekend in Devon and Cornwall you may be hard-pushed to find a vacancy at the last minute. The answer again is simply to use a little thought. If you must take your holiday at the peak of the summer rush, then find somewhere other than the popular areas of the West Country or the Scottish Highlands. Ninety-five per cent of land in Britain is still classified as agricultural—and site possibilities just across the Channel are even better than over here.

Many British sites (including an excellent chain in some of our beautiful forest land owned and administered by the Forestry Commission) do not accept advance bookings, so caravanning can still be something of a day-to-day adventure at the most popular times of year.

Forestry Commission sites are in my opinion some of the country's best (and cheapest), but that's mainly because I'd rather be surrounded by fields and forests than bingo halls and snack bars. Whether you want seclusion, crowds and supermarkets, or simple facilities and a village atmosphere, there are sites at home and abroad to suit you. Britain is still short of caravan sites, but numbers are increasing and they're undoubtedly getting better. The position is not as hopeless as many pessimists might have you believe.

These then are just a few reasons why I believe caravanning could be the answer to your holiday needs, in the same way that it was the answer to mine. It would be foolish to pretend that everyone likes caravanning—if they did there wouldn't be enough room on Britain's roads or sites for us all!—but if the initial interest is there, read on. It could be a lot simpler than you think.

British caravans are tough. In a recent endurance test staged at Silverstone race circuit, this Ford Escort RS2000/CI Sprint covered 1,001 miles at an average 53·56 mph and the British Leyland Mini, towing a similar caravan, covered 901 miles in the same time at an average 48·15 mph

Pioneers of the 'go-as-you-please' holiday—with servants

Modern luxury caravanning on a peaceful site run by the Forestry Commission

Chapter 2
What kind of caravan?

Assuming you and your family have decided in principle that you would like a caravan, the first obvious question is, what sort? I'll be dealing in Chapter 3 with the types of van that are available, but before you make any decision on the kind you'll need — let alone its make — there are certain factors you must consider carefully.

First, you must assess your needs, deciding how many people the van must sleep, whether or not you will carry your own toilet or rely on site facilities, etc; you have to consider the financial angle, deciding where you are going to obtain the money for your purchase; you must consider very carefully the towing capability of your car (see Chapter 6); and you'll

have to come to some decision about where you are going to store the van when you are not actually on holiday.

Don't be put off the idea of caravanning just because you have a large family. It's quite surprising just how comfortably a big family can live in such a confined space — provided everything is put back in its proper place after use. If nothing else, caravanning will teach you and your family to be tidy! One thing that surprises newcomers to caravanning is that a tourer sleeping as many as five or six may cost no more than a similar-size model sleeping only two; in fact the reverse is often true, for it is cheaper for the manufacturer to build in bed bases and mattresses than to fill the space with complicated cabinetry and storage cupboards.

British caravan makers export their products throughout the world and, what's more, they have a reputation for good design and low cost. You'll find few, if any, imported tourers in most showrooms, and those you do come across will be significantly more expensive than those from the home industry.

Standard features in all modern tourers include dining and sleeping facilities, somewhere to cook and wash-up, and somewhere to store your clothes and bedding. There is almost no end to the number of luxury fittings that can be added — but make sure the van you choose will house all the family comfortably without being too much of a strain on your car

Choosing a caravan

Once you have some idea of the layouts and features found in today's caravans – by visiting exhibitions, studying magazines, etc – and have decided roughly what you need, you shouldn't have too much trouble in finding a new or used van that meets your requirements. Naturally, as a general rule anyway, the bigger the caravan you want the more you'll have to pay for it. Of course this rule of thumb applies only to tourers of similar quality. You can find really luxurious tourers with bodies no longer than 12 feet that cost far more than 16-footers with a more basic specification.

If you have no idea of what the inside of a modern tourer looks like – and some makes in particular have changed considerably within the last few years – then go along to at least two or three local dealers and browse around the stock.

When you are looking for a caravan, make a realistic assessment of the maximum size and weight your car can tow – Chapter 6 will help here. Don't necessarily look for the biggest van the car manufacturer says it can tow, and don't always rely on the caravan salesman's recommendation; he may have a vested interest in selling you a bigger caravan than you need or can comfortably tow

Finding a dealer

How *do* you find dealers—and, more important, the reputable ones? First, write for a list of accredited dealers, manufacturers and equipment suppliers to the National Caravan Council. This is a trade body that represents all sides of the British caravan industry and publishes annually a full list of members. You will find its address at the back of this book.

The idea of going to at least two or three dealers is that many of them are tied to a particular manufacturer (or manufacturers) and at this early stage it's best for you to see as many different types and styles of van as possible.

Even if you intend buying a second-hand van—maybe through a classified advertisement—it will pay you to visit a few showrooms and see some new vans to give you an idea of what to look for.

What to look for

You'll find that the quality of furnishings and fittings varies quite a lot from make to make and from one price range to another, but the design ideas remain basically the same. All modern tourers come with adequate cooking and washing facilities, together with places to eat and sleep and storage space for clothes, bedding and food. You'll find that the bed arrangements vary, that some vans are fitted with toilet compartments and others aren't, and that kitchens are positioned variously at the front, back or sides of the tourer; in Chapter 3 we'll take a look at the pros and cons of these designs.

All caravans have some form of interior lighting—gas or, more commonly these days, electric—and almost certainly there will be space for a small refrigerator if one isn't fitted already.

On the technical side you should check that the caravan is fitted with all the necessary road lights and reflectors, a braking system that works in conjunction with the towing car, and a towing coupling. In fact the caravan you buy, if new at least, will be ready for the road once you have installed your own personal gear—though of course your car must first be fitted with a towing bracket and an outlet socket for electricity to power the van's road-lighting circuit.

Many caravanners start off with a used van and this is not a bad idea. Basically it is true to say that there is less risk in buying a used caravan than a used car because there is far less that could go wrong. The chassis and undergear are relatively simple pieces of machinery and an hour or so going over the interior of the van to make sure the fittings aren't too badly worn should tell you whether or not you are getting a bargain. If

Most caravans, like this Lynton, have their kitchens positioned at the centre. The usual arrangement is to have a two-burner hotplate, grill and sink unit, though an increasing number of models nowadays also have fridges as standard equipment. Fridges can almost always be fitted as optional extras when they are not part of the standard specification

you are in any doubt, get a qualified fitter to check over the gas system or, if you want a full report on the van's condition, the Automobile Association will vet it for a nominal fee in the same way as they check over used cars.

Two important things to bear in mind when you are selecting a caravan, new or used, are that you will need a van that will sleep all the family in comfort (remembering that a child may well grow by several feet within the life of your van) and that there must be enough room and weight tolerance to cope with all the family's clothes, food and bedding. You will be surprised just how many berths some caravan manufacturers can squeeze into quite a small bodyshell, but if you are attracted to this sort of van make sure the design is sound.

Another very important thing to know is the van's weight. Ask the dealer (or, in the case of a private sale, find out from the manufacturer) details of the van's 'ex-works' empty weight and the maximum weight to which it can be loaded. It is important that the loaded weight should not be higher than the kerbside (empty) weight of your tow car, and, just as important, that the difference between the ex-works and maximum trailer weight allows you enough leeway for food, bedding and clothing for all the family. It's no good buying a 12-foot van that will sleep you, your wife and all the children if the maximum laden weight of the van restricts you to only 1 hundredweight of personal effects for the whole family.

Make a note of the van's overall dimensions. Remember, you've got to find somewhere to store it at home or else pay someone else to look after it while it isn't in use. And continental car-ferry operators work out their charges on the basis of length . . . so an extra few inches can mean a lot of extra cost if you're a regular traveller abroad.

Away from it all in Glennevis this compact 12ft 5in van sleeps four, has an optional fifth bunk and two separate sleeping areas

Financing

The financial side of buying a caravan needs careful consideration as, after your house and car, the tourer is likely to be the most expensive single item you'll ever buy. When you sit down with pencil and paper and work out how much you can afford to spend on your first venture into caravanning, don't forget to allow enough for getting your car ready for towing (that means adding a towing bracket, electricity socket and maybe mirrors — see Chapter 6) and for buying essential extras like bottled gas, regulator, sleeping bags, etc (see Chapter 8). These are all reasonably constant amounts, whereas you can vary the amount to be spent on the van itself.

Most of us, when buying a house, a car or whatever, usually end up paying that little bit more than we anticipated, so set your sights a little lower than the maximum amount you can afford. Then, when you visit the dealer's showroom, see what is available within that price range.

Once you have reckoned your financial limit, you next have to set about raising the capital — assuming you are not one of those lucky few who already have the cash tucked away in the bank! The caravan dealer will be only too happy to arrange hire purchase facilities for you (after all, he makes a profit on it) but you may well do better to go to one of the big finance houses or to see your bank manager (who is there to give you just this sort of advice) about a private loan or overdraft.

While we are on the subject of money, many prospective caravanners ask whether their vans will depreciate in value very quickly — is there the sort of fall-off in value that you would expect with, for example, a car? Until the very recent past it was a fairly accurate estimate to say that touring vans depreciated at around 10 per cent a year, but the demand for used vans over the last couple of years (and especially since the introduction of VAT) has been so great that this figure has been drastically reduced. Just how long this situation will last is anyone's guess. There have been cases of tourers two or three years old selling for almost as much as their original cost. It's something to look out for if you are in the market for a second-hand van — check the original selling price with the manufacturer.

Chiefly because a caravan was considered to be a dwelling place, purchase tax was never levied on tourers. When Britain switched over to the VAT system, however, the government saw fit to extend this to caravans — with the result that all new caravans rose substantially in price. If you buy a new caravan from a dealer nowadays, you pay VAT on it; if you buy a used van from a private individual not registered for VAT you pay no tax; and if you buy a used van from a dealer, you pay VAT on *his profit margin only*. The same law applies to second-hand car sales, but there have been cases reported of car dealers charging tax on the purchase price rather than their profit. I haven't heard of any similar case in the caravan industry, but it's something to watch out for.

The question of storage

There are several advantages to storing your caravan at home if this is at all possible. Although you are not allowed to use the van as an extension of your house, you can use it on the odd occasion when you need to put up an unexpected guest. You will also avoid storage charges, which can be very high, by keeping the van at home. Keeping it at home will cost you nothing other than, say, the cost of altering a hedge or laying a concrete hard-standing. And of course it will be handy for you to carry out regular cleaning, airing the mattresses and doing what little maintenance is required on the undergear.

You should aim to store your caravan alongside or behind the house. If this is impossible, you should realize from the start that you will have to find storage space elsewhere. Remember also that some houses are subject to covenants that forbid the standing of caravans on their land — you'll have to check your house deeds on this point.

If you do have to find somewhere to store your van, have a word with the dealer selling it to you — most caravan retailers can provide you with storage space or put you in touch with someone who can. The Caravan Club also keeps a list of storage addresses.

The motor caravan

Although this book is written especially for prospective touring caravanners, by which I mean those people who tow touring caravans behind their cars, perhaps here I should briefly mention the motor caravan.

Modern motor vans come in a great variety of shapes and sizes and in their equipment they are designed along similar lines to trailer vans. The advantage of the motor caravan is of course that you tour with only one vehicle, but unless you choose a very big one you'll have less living space than that offered by even the smallest trailer model. Motor vans are expensive but, provided you don't mind driving a vehicle of this size for everyday transport, cost no more than a car and trailer caravan together.

Although less roomy than a trailer van the motor caravan is obviously ideal for a solitary fishing trip

Chapter 3
Caravans today

Caravan dimensions

The smallest size of trailer caravan easily available in Britain these days has a body length of around 8 feet 6 inches; the biggest a body length of something over 22 feet. Between these two extremes there is a whole host of variations in interior layout, external body shape and colouring — something to suit 99 per cent of prospective buyers. The most popular sizes are 12- to 16-footers. And it's between these sort of figures that you'll find the largest selection. There are also plenty of 10- and 11-footers around, but below 10 feet and above 16 feet the choice is not so good.

Body widths normally lie somewhere, usually about midway, between 6 and 7 feet, so in most cases you can reckon on the trailer being a few inches wider than your car on each side. There are a few models on the market with widths of less than 6 feet — usually small-size vans intended for the smallest tow cars — but these are the exception rather than the rule. By extending the body width to over 6 feet, however, the manufacturer can fit in beds either lengthways or crossways.

Average heights are 8 feet or more — taller than you might at first think, though it's obvious when you consider that there must be 6 feet of headroom inside and room for the undergear below floor level. Bear this in mind if you intend storing your caravan at home, especially in a garage or carport; few garages offer this sort of height unless they are especially designed to do so.

Caravan construction

Axles

Almost all British tourers have a single axle – one centrally located wheel on either side. A few of the bigger and heavier vans have two axles, with of course two wheels on either side, and where the centres of the two adjacent wheels are no more than 33 inches apart (which is almost invariably the case) this is defined as a 'close-coupled twin-axle chassis'. (This is a legal definition, and the law applying to trailers with a wheel at each corner is different.)

The number of British-made vans with close-coupled twin axles is very small; the idea is more popular on the Continent. Unless the caravan is very heavy the idea has little to recommend it, as it doesn't necessarily make the van any more stable, but it does make it much more difficult to manhandle because as you try to turn the trailer you are inevitably scrubbing one set of tyres. If you see one of the few close-coupled caravans on the market and it takes your eye – they do have a stylish appearance – make sure that you really need one of this size before going ahead.

The chassis

All caravans, no matter what their body construction, are built up from a chassis of welded steel angle and channel. Added to the chassis are the central axle (or axles), a suitable suspension system, wheels and a braking mechanism. Most caravans built over the past few years have independent suspension, usually by leaf or coil springs, or occasionally by torsion bars or compressed rubber units. Only an expert caravanner who has towed many trailers over thousands of miles could tell the difference in the handling of differently equipped vans. The suspension requires very little maintenance other than occasional oiling of springs (see Chapter 10).

Brakes

On virtually all British caravans the brakes are activated by an overrun mechanism that comes into operation whenever the tow car slows down. The car and caravan are connected rigidly at the coupling and, when the tow car slows down, the action of the caravan trying to 'overtake' the car pushes back a piston in the coupling head. This in turn is connected to a rod linkage that pulls on the drum brakes at the caravan wheels.

Various attempts have been made to introduce electric and hydraulic brakes for caravans, but only a tiny number of vans was ever sold with either system in Britain. Electric brakes are widely used in the United States where the giant 'travel trailer' can weigh as much as 3 tons on the road, but with the sort of weights we are concerned with, electric braking systems give little or no advantage. Hydraulic systems are available on the accessory market, but they are expensive and the increased performance is probably of limited importance for normal day-to-day caravanning.

Tyres

Although radial-ply tyres are now standard equipment on many cars and are a popular option with even more, you will almost certainly find that your caravan is fitted with the cross-ply variety. It is not dangerous (or illegal) to tow a cross-ply-tyred caravan with a car fitted with radials. Caravan makers use cross-ply tyres because they are cheaper and because the two principal advantages of radials – their long life and good roadholding – are not really applicable to the lowish mileage and slow,

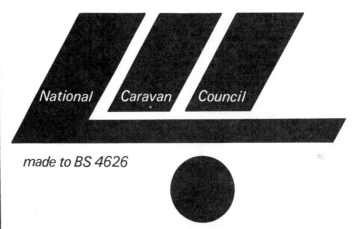

made to BS 4626

There is a British Standard for touring caravans – BS4626 – which covers a multitude of design features from insulation to brake efficiency; copies of it can be obtained from the British Standards Institute in London. Virtually all caravan manufacturers in Britain are members of the National Caravan Council and attach this special badge to all tourers that conform to BS4626

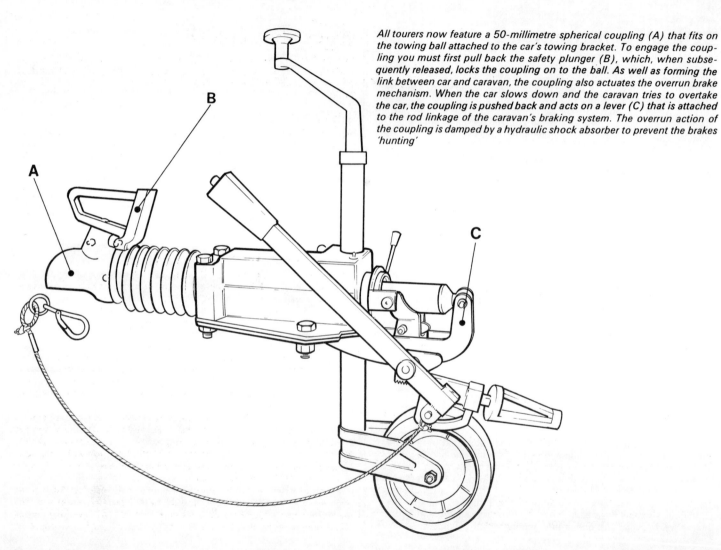

All tourers now feature a 50-millimetre spherical coupling (A) that fits on the towing ball attached to the car's towing bracket. To engage the coupling you must first pull back the safety plunger (B), which, when subsequently released, locks the coupling on to the ball. As well as forming the link between car and caravan, the coupling also actuates the overrun brake mechanism. When the car slows down and the caravan tries to overtake the car, the coupling is pushed back and acts on a lever (C) that is attached to the rod linkage of the caravan's braking system. The overrun action of the coupling is damped by a hydraulic shock absorber to prevent the brakes 'hunting'

B

A

C

careful driving that most caravans are subjected to. Some caravanners maintain that radials are positively unsuitable for caravans because their supple walls increase instability.

No British caravan manufacturer sends his vans out equipped with spare wheels. Admittedly on-the-road tyre failures are pretty rare these days, but even so I should like to be prepared for all emergencies – especially if, for instance, I was heading across the Continent. I think a spare wheel is a sound investment, and those caravanners who disagree should always carry with them a tyre repair kit and know how to use it. If you want a spare wheel for your caravan, order it from your dealer; don't visit scrap yards trying to find an old car wheel that will fit – you won't find one.

The coupling

One of the most important aspects of caravan chassis design concerns the part you attach to your car – the coupling. Britain and the rest of Europe use a standard 50-millimetre-diameter coupling, with the towing ball attached to the rear of the car and an inverted cup on the trailer.

Years ago Britain used a 2-inch coupling and, though there is very little difference in the two sizes, it would be dangerous to try to force a 50-millimetre coupling head over a 2-inch ball, or let a 2-inch coupling fit loosely on a 50-millimetre ball. Unless you have a car fitted with a very old towing bracket, or unless you tow a very old caravan, the situation is never likely to arise, but it is as well to know how to tell the difference between the two. First take a look at the side of the coupling head: if it is the correct, commonly used size it will have '50mm' in raised type on the side. Similarly, a 50-millimetre towing ball has a flat surface, about the diameter of a one-penny piece, on top with the figure '50' or '50mm' or 'ISO 50' stamped on it.

The body

Body designs vary, of course, from manufacturer to manufacturer, in the same way as car designs vary. The most commonly used material for caravan exteriors is aluminium sheeting, usually pre-finished or occasionally spray-painted. Some new models incorporate panels of glass fibre or vacuum-formed plastics and there are a few models that have bodies made completely of glass fibre. In most cases where these plastic or glass materials are used, it is in the form of front and/or rear end panels or, in the case of a few makes, roof and floor panels.

Windows are not normally made of safety glass – which is one reason why the law forbids touring caravanners to carry passengers in their vans.

Inside the caravan

Caravan interiors are usually finished plywood these days, with a photo-finish or applied material finish. In very expensive vans you will still find natural wood veneers on the interior surfaces.

Insulation

Between the interior wood and the exterior aluminium or whatever, the caravan walls contain an insulating material – usually glass-fibre wool or, occasionally, foamed-in plastics. The insulation is also carried across the roof, though not all vans have floor insulation. If you intend caravanning in winter or in cold climates, floor insulation is a worthwhile extra if it isn't fitted as standard; you can order it to be put in during manufacture or, if you are buying a second-hand van, you can carry out a do-it-yourself job with expanded polystyrene sheeting protected underneath by a layer of stout polythene sheeting.

Seating and sleeping

Inside the caravan, as I mentioned in Chapter 1, you'll find all the facilities required for you and your family to live comfortably during your holiday – though this excludes personal bedding, cooking utensils, etc. Perhaps the most important of the internal fitments is the seating and sleeping arrangement. I have put these two together because in a touring caravan one converts to the other.

Basically there are three types of bed provided in tourers: the dinette arrangement; the canvas bunk (sometimes called a 'stretcher bunk' or 'roll-away bunk'); and the pullman bunk, which has a hard base with a mattress on top. The dinette is so called because in daytime you use it as your dining area, so although not every caravan has bunk beds they all feature some sort of dinette.

In most tourers the dinette comprises two settees, set at the front or rear end of the van, with a table hooked on to the end wall and supported at the other end by a drop-down leg. Each of the settees seats two people (sometimes three at a pinch) and the table is big enough to hold a meal for four. If the van sleeps more than four adults, you may also find a similar or smaller dinette at the other end.

To make a dinette like this up into a double bed, you first fold up the table leg and unhook the table from the wall. You then lower it to the level of the locker tops beneath the settee cushions, where it should just fill the gap – possibly with the help of another extra piece of wood supplied.

Then remove the settee backrests and use them to fill in the table area — and you have a bed for two adults set across the width of the van.

Some caravans (particularly some of the more expensive models) have longer settees that you can use as single beds just as they are, though in many cases they can be converted to a double bed. Sometimes you'll find that the backrest of a 6-foot settee designed for use as a single bed is hinged at the top, so that it too can act as a single bed when it is fixed in the raised position. This is a pullman bunk.

Stretcher bunks are sometimes permanently fixed at one side, but sometimes they are completely removable so that they can be stored out of sight (for example, behind a settee backrest) during the daytime. Normally they consist of two tubular metal poles with canvas or nylon stretched between them; the ends of the poles fit into metal cups or wooden slots built into the caravan wall. They're quite safe, though you may be a little wary of them at first! If a stretcher bunk is 6 feet or so long, you can assume it has been put there for use by an adult and it will take your

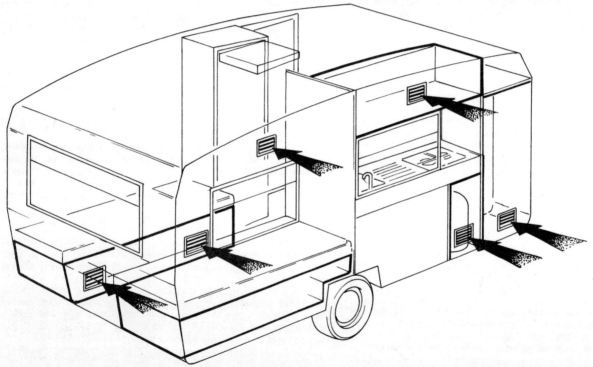

Lockers for bedding are almost always provided in dinette and settee bases. They should be well ventilated to the inside of the caravan, not to the outside. Food is usually stored in lockers beneath the kitchen unit or attached to the wall at roof level above it; the main food storage cupboard should be vented to the outside. In caravans that have an interior gas bottle locker adequate ventilation to the outside of the van is essential

weight easily. Sometimes manufacturers fit shorter bunks designed specially for children, but this is not very common in trailer vans.

So much then for the beds. You will of course have to supply your own blankets and sheets or, better still, sleeping bags, but I'll deal further with these items in Chapter 8.

The dinette

With your dinette set up for a daytime meal you'll find that the table top has a coating of melamine laminate. This is because few caravanners get through a holiday without having to put down a hot plate or saucepan on the table, and natural wood would soon be marked. A heat-resistant, wipe-clean laminate surface will save time and tempers.

In many caravans there is room to store the table in a wardrobe or toilet compartment or behind a settee when you aren't using it, but in some models the table is always set up or in use as part of the bed base. If you think you'll be spending quite a bit of time in your van in the evenings (if, for instance, you have young children and will need to spend time inside after they have been put to bed), it is handy to have somewhere set aside for table storage; it can take up a lot of room in your 'lounge' if you want to use it simply for lounging.

The dinette converts into a double bed when the table is lowered to bench height. The backrest cushions fill in as a mattress

The kitchen

By far the most common position for a touring caravan kitchen is at the centre of the van, along one of the walls. This is sensible because the kitchen features a lot of heavy items (cooker, water storage, maybe a fridge and a lot of tinned food) and this is best kept over the axle line.

Some vans have their kitchens across the front wall; this is all right provided it doesn't make the van too nose-heavy when loaded and provided the taller kitchen units don't obstruct the view through the caravan's windows when driving (see Chapter 6). Not many caravans have rear-end kitchens, but in those that do you must load your food and kitchen equipment sensibly so that the van doesn't become too heavy at the rear.

Sinks may be plastic or stainless steel and are usually (though not always) supplied with a small draining area. Few British vans have waste-water holding tanks – normally water from the sink runs out through a flexible pipe to a point under the van, where you have to stand a waste-water bucket.

If you want an oven, you may be able to fit one as an extra – only on a few vans is it standard.

Water storage

Water may be stored in loose containers (which may or may not be supplied) or your van may have a built-in water tank. If the tank is built in, the van must of course also feature some sort of pump to draw water up to the sink; but if you rely on loose water carriers, a water pump may be standard or an optional extra. The most common types of water pump are manually operated, either by hand or foot, but there are a number of low-voltage electric pumps on the market (see page 58).

The toilet

You may decide that you are going to carry and use your own chemical toilet all the time – Chapter 9 deals with caravan sanitation – or on the other hand you may decide you're going to stay only on sites that provide toilet facilities. Naturally if you make the first choice you'll want a caravan with a toilet compartment, but even if you aren't intending to use a chemical toilet, a compartment for one can be useful.

For a start it makes an ideal changing room – small, but it saves having to draw all the curtains if you run back from the beach to change from your swimsuit. Many toilet compartments in the latest vans have attractive tiled walls and small washbasins, sometimes with their own water pump

One recent development in the design of touring caravan equipment is the one-piece combined cooker, sink and drainer. The unit combines the usual two boiling rings and grill with the sink unit, and the whole is normally finished in stainless steel

and water supply. And you can even install a shower inside a caravan toilet compartment! But check that the separate compartment in the van of your choice is the right size—whatever purpose you intend it for.

Carpeting

Most vans have carpeted floors, which are warm to step on to when you get out of bed and which help insulate the van. They even look nice in the showroom! That may sound a little cynical, but with a little experience you'll soon realize that a fitted carpet is a little impractical when all and sundry tread mud from the farm or sand from the beach into it every time they come into the van. Check the quality of the carpet in one or two models and try to choose one that looks as though it will stand some rough treatment.

Storage space

Apart from cupboards under the sink and cooker, which are intended for food storage and kitchen utensils, caravans have lockers beneath the seating to take care of bedding. Food-storage cupboards should be vented to the outside of the van (though any vents should have proper meshing to prevent insects getting in), but bedding-storage lockers should be vented to the inside and not the outside, as this could make your bedding wet during a storm.

A proper wardrobe should be provided for clothes that have to be hung up, and there should be other lockers—normally at head height at the sides or ends of the van—for other items such as folded clothes. These roof lockers will have sliding doors or, more probably, front flaps that lift up or drop down. In the case of lift-up locker fronts, make sure there is something to hold them in the open position.

Chapter 4
Hiring before you buy

Many people thinking of taking up trailer caravanning hire a tourer before actually buying their own because it is a good way for them and the family to see whether they will like caravan holidays. It is a good idea, certainly. But there is one snag that puts some people off: before you can tow any caravan, hired or otherwise, you must spend a fair sum of money having your car fitted with a towing bracket and electric socket.

Unfortunately there is no way round this; there is no sort of clip-on towing bracket that the hire company can attach to your car for the duration of the hire period and then take back with the van. So before you consider hiring a van, consider the cost of adapting your car. Having done so, you may still be surprised at how inexpensive a caravan holiday can be in terms of the freedom and scope it offers.

Some people hire a caravan every holiday instead of buying, but of course there are a great many who will hire a van first with the intention of buying their own later. If this is your idea and you have a particular make and model in mind, it's worth visiting several different hire companies to see if you can hire the van that's taken your fancy.

The cost

The cost involved in actually borrowing a tourer from one of the hire companies varies according to a number of factors: the size of the van, the time of year you want it and, of course, how long you want it for.

You will probably have to leave some sort of deposit at the time you make your hire booking, and this may either form part of the hire charge (i.e. the deposit sum is deducted from your final bill) or it may form no part but just be a deposit against breakages or damage.

How to choose

Make sure before the salesman tries to talk you into having a particular model that you know the kerbside weight of your car and its towing limit. You can read what significance these figures have in Chapters 6 and 7.

The size and type of caravan you require naturally depends on the number of people going on holiday and the car you intend to tow it with, but of course you are more restricted when hiring than when buying because not every model of every make finds its way on to the hire fleet.

As you might expect, hire companies concentrate on the lower-priced caravan ranges—in the same way as few car hire companies have Rolls Royces or Mercedes on their fleets. They specialize in the most popular makes and sizes—and this usually means vans 11 to 16 feet long, designed for average-size families rather than single couples or large numbers.

If you want a van that will sleep more than the average number of people, you may have to shop around or find a company associated with a retail outlet (many are) that is willing to put an extra van on the hire fleet. In this case you may have to pay an additional hire fee.

Check the van and contents

When you collect the van, you should check over its condition inside and out, and point out to the hire company any points that are not right. If, for instance, there is a scratch on one side, make sure you tell the person concerned before starting your holiday. If it's discovered only when you return, you may be held responsible.

You should be given an inventory of the van's contents. But before leaving with your van, go through it and make sure everything on the list is present and in working condition. Again, if you return later with items missing or broken, you may be held responsible.

Refunds

If for some reason you cut short your holiday and decide to return your van after, say, ten days instead of fourteen, don't expect to get any of your hire fee returned. If you entered into a contract with the company to hire their caravan for fourteen days, they are under no legal obligation to return any of your money. Of course some firms are more sympathetic than others if your return is forced by illness or other unforeseen circumstances, but no company will want to give you back your money if you come back early because you decided you'd rather stay in a hotel or because it rained all the time you were away.

Insurance

Make sure your car insurers know you are going to tow a caravan—it's important that they should know, though in most cases it won't affect either your insurance cover or the premium payable. The hired caravan should be insured by the company from which you borrow it, and the sum involved is almost invariably part of the hire charge. You may, however, have to pay an additional hire fee (to cover extra insurance, among other things) if you intend to take the van out of the country.

Going abroad

Many people take hired caravans abroad, but don't do so unless you have made it quite clear to the company from which you hire. Although the fees may be higher, it's not worth taking the risk of going abroad without the proper insurance cover.

If you want to visit the Continent, it's also worth seeing whether the ferry company involved runs its own hire scheme; several of them do, and there are usually advantageous terms for users of their ferries. The snag often is that you have to pick up your van this side of the Channel—and then pay the return fare for your extra vehicle. To overcome this problem you can hire on the other side of the Channel (many continental hire firms advertise in British caravan magazines), but then you are stuck with the problem of getting across the Channel with all the clothes and equipment you are going to need for your holiday.

Your first caravan holiday

To give caravanning a fair trial before deciding whether or not to buy, you should hire your van for at least a couple of weeks—though maybe two separate weeks with different types of van are better than a fortnight in a single model. Make sure you do plenty of towing—to see how your car shapes up under the extra load and to make sure you too are happy with the idea. And another thing, by taking your first holiday out of season, avoiding the peak holiday months of July and August, you'll enjoy two benefits: lower hire rates and less congestion—both on the roads and at the caravan sites you choose.

Most companies that deal in caravan hire can also provide all the extras, such as sleeping bags, cooking utensils—even crockery and cutlery if you wish. These things are not normally provided in many cases, so you will have to pay extra, but it shouldn't cost you very much at all. It is probably better to pay a bit more than either to have the bother of making up sheets and blankets each night or to have to buy sleeping bags. And you certainly won't want to take your best china tea set caravanning, so if you don't have any picnic crockery this is worth hiring too. You will be expected to supply personal items such as towels and sleeping-bag liners.

Naturally you'll want gas for cooking, and maybe also for lighting and a refrigerator; your van will be equipped with one full cylinder (maybe even two) but you'll be expected to pay for any refilling that becomes necessary while you are on holiday. If you're a small family and use gas only for cooking, refilling may not even be necessary.

Once you have had the necessary towing bracket and electric socket fitted to your car (or have fitted it yourself), make sure all the bolts are tight—they can sometimes loosen up a little after the first few hundred miles—and make certain that all the electrical connections are right. The

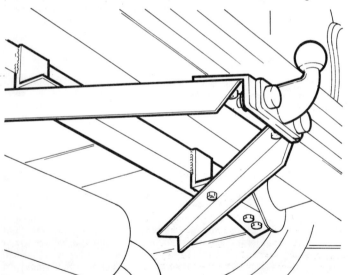

The design and manufacture of towing brackets is a specialized job—especially in these days of unitary car body construction, when the towing bracket designer must make sure he picks up sufficiently strong points underneath the car

best way to do this is to try to find a friend who already has a caravan or trailer and connect that to your car. Try rear lights, indicators and brake lights *individually and together* and if there's anything amiss, get it sorted out. You don't want to turn up to collect your holiday van and find out then that the brake lights flash on and off with your car indicators!

If the hired van is going to be your first taste of towing, make this clear at the time you collect your van (if not before). Often the salesman will be able to give you a lot of useful advice and will take more care in showing you how to hitch up the van and set it up on site. Whether you are an old hand or not, get the salesman to go over any points on which you aren't clear. It's his job to make sure you are entirely happy with the van and there's no reason why you shouldn't make him earn his money. If he's sensible, he too will realize that it's better for you to know how everything works than to risk you breaking something.

Provided the company isn't too busy at the time of your visit, they may let you take the car and caravan out for a short spin with someone to show you the ropes, in any case you'll find that after a few miles on the road you'll soon gain confidence if the car and van are properly matched.

Buying second-hand from a dealer

Most of the big caravan sales companies operate hire fleets, and it's quite usual for them to renew their stock once a year—usually around October. Ex-hire caravans are often a good buy as they are usually sold off well below their initial purchase price and they may well have had only a few months' use. Unlike hire cars they are usually well treated too.

Sometimes the savings can be as much as 20 per cent, and often those people who have hired vans during the season are given preference when, at the end of the summer, the dealer sells his stock. If you return from your holiday thoroughly satisfied with the van, ask the company what happens to hire models; you may be able to reserve that particular one.

Borrowing from friends

Finally a word about hiring or borrowing a touring caravan from friends, and about lending your van to others. This is all very well provided you take the necessary steps to note the condition of the van before and after it has been lent—as you would if you were dealing with a big company. Don't accept your friends' word that 'she's insured whoever is using her'—many people come unstuck that way, so make sure you see the policy.

Chapter 5
When you have bought your caravan

Dealer's responsibilities

Once you have found the caravan of your choice, you will naturally want to collect it as soon as possible. If it's a second-hand model, there will be no problem about delivery, and with a new van bought from a dealer there is usually little delay, though with some models you may have to wait a few weeks for delivery. The problem is certainly not as bad as in the car industry, where production rates are a lot higher, but you have a greater choice of exterior colour, trim, etc.

Whether your van is new or used, if you are buying it from a dealer it should be in good working order when you collect it. The dealer should have given it a thorough pre-delivery inspection. In the case of new tourers the manufacturers take into account the time and work involved when they calculate their dealer profits and you will not have to pay anything extra for this check-over.

So when you pick up your van the tyre pressures should be set correctly; the braking system should have been adjusted and all the equipment checked to make sure it is in good working order. Caravan dealers are busy people, so give the company a few days' warning once you have decided on which day to collect your new van; you can then be sure all the work has been done and your van is ready for the road. If you asked for any extras to be fitted (water pump, heater, fridge, etc) mention this too, just in case anything hasn't been attended to.

One thing that's absolutely essential to have before you set out on the road – but one thing that cannot be provided in advance – is a rear number plate. The numbers and letters must naturally correspond to those on your car's registration plates; caravans are not registered separately and caravanners pay no extra road tax. There is also no official document like a log book issued with a trailer van. The only documents you are likely to be handed are the manufacturer's warranty cards and explanatory booklets.

The laws regarding the size, shape and colour of caravan registration plates are the same as those applied to the rear number plate of a car. For safety's sake it is definitely worth while to fit the rear of the trailer with the yellow reflective type of plate, though in fact this is not a legal requirement as it is with new cars. It is also not a legal requirement for the caravan number plate to be of the same type as those on the car.

If the dealer is to supply and fit the number plate, don't forget to give him details of the tow car's registration in advance; if no mention is made of the number plate when you place your order, then you must assume you are supposed to supply one. If you can't get a proper metal plate made up before going to collect your van, you can use one of the cheap stick-on types initially. These are available from car accessory shops and also from many caravan dealers.

Your responsibilities

Before collecting your van it is of course your responsibility to make sure your car is fitted with a proper towing bracket, electric socket and, if necessary for a clear rear view, additional driving mirrors. Full details about these fittings are given in Chapter 6.

Insurance

Before towing anything you must inform your car insurance company. It's better to put this in writing and get it acknowledged than to rely on a simple phone call or verbal confirmation from the broker; a brief note to the insurer's head office or your insurance broker should suffice.

In fact if you look carefully at your insurance policy you may find that you are covered for trailer towing already, usually with the proviso that you aren't doing it for financial gain. But if you are in any doubt, make sure you clear this matter up before going to collect your van.

Even if your policy doesn't automatically cover you for towing, it shouldn't cost very much to have this extra risk included. In my own case the insurance company simply noted the fact and didn't charge any extra premium at all. Once you have informed the insurance company and they have accepted the risk, you have satisfied the law's demands. If you are involved in an accident and the trailer damages any person or his property, the case will be treated in the same manner as if the car itself had been involved in the collision.

But even if you have comprehensive cover for the car this does not extend to cover damage sustained by your caravan. You will have to take out another special policy to cover accidental damage to your van, and normally this will also cover loss or damage in the event of fire, theft or any other disaster.

Policies are issued by all the major insurance groups and provided your caravan is of a reasonably well-known make rather than a one-off model, you should have no difficulty in getting cover.

Preparing to drive off

Details of the different sorts of towing mirrors available to motorists are given elsewhere in this book, but there's a good chance that at the time when you pick up your van you won't have made up your mind which sort will suit you and your car best. Do make sure that before setting out on the road you have adequate ways of knowing what's going on behind you. There are clip-on door mirrors which, though quite expensive, seem to give very good results with all outfits, and there are extension mirrors to fit over your existing wing mirrors for a wider view; these are relatively inexpensive.

Unless you have towed a trailer before, you probably won't be familiar with the coupling mechanism and the way it works. Get the salesman to show you – several times if necessary – how to hitch the car and caravan together; and later, when you have an hour to spare, take the van somewhere quiet and practise reversing the car up to it until you can stop with the towing ball within an inch or two of the coupling.

Once you have mastered the coupling-up procedure, plug in the electric socket. (You should have remembered to check the car's outlet socket

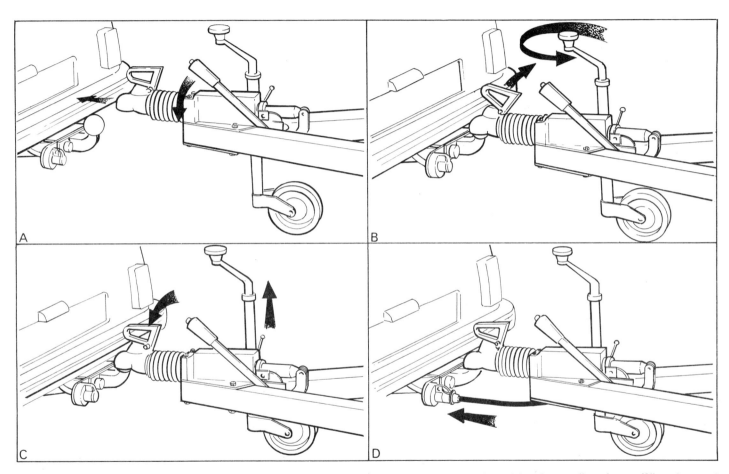

With the car manoeuvred into such a position that the ball is as near as possible to the coupling – something you will master with practice – release the caravan handbrake and guide the coupling to a position directly over the ball. Wind down the jockey-wheel stem and guide the coupling on to the ball, at the same time raising the coupling plunger. When the coupling is fitted on the ball, release the plunger and make sure the coupling has locked securely. Raise the jockey wheel and lock it in the uppermost position, then plug in the electrical connection before going along to pick up the van.) Safe in the knowledge that your car is wired up properly, switch on the side lights and make sure both front and rear lights and the number-plate light on the van light up. Then, with the ignition switch on, try the indicators on each side. With the indicators still flashing, put your foot on the car's brake and get someone to tell you if the van's brake lights come on too. If they do, then try all the lights again individually.

Having made sure the electric plug is home securely and that the caravan coupling is locked on the towing ball of your car, you have only to raise the jockey wheel (that's the small wheel at the front of the van) and lock it in the 'up' position, then release the caravan handbrake. Do make sure that the jockey wheel is up as far as it will go, or it may hit the ground if you go over a pothole. Similarly, make sure that you have tightened its locking screw properly, or it may suddenly drop while you are going along, and then buckle.

You can wind any excess seven-core cable in the car/caravan electric lead round the jockey-wheel stem; but make certain that the lead is left neither too loose nor too tight. If it's too tight, the plug will pull out when you go round the first corner; if it's too loose, it may drag along the ground or get caught up.

Towing your first caravan

Towing a caravan is not at all difficult but it does demand a lot of concentration, particularly when you are new to it. No doubt you will feel a little nervous when you go to collect your first van, although it's surprising how soon you get used to the extra weight and length. But you should never get *so* used to it that you forget it's there.

Having a caravan on the back of your car naturally affects its performance in all sorts of ways. Provided your car is in good condition and you have chosen the right size and type of caravan, you should have no serious trouble—and if you do Chapter 6 should help you sort that out. The first thing you'll notice is that both acceleration and braking are affected. Naturally your car has to work harder to get the outfit on the move, and once you have gained speed the brakes have more weight to stop—though, if they are correctly adjusted, the caravan brakes should play a very great part in bringing the trailer to rest.

Braking efficiency tests carried out with solo cars and with the same cars hitched to properly adjusted caravans show only a small difference in the retardation attainable, but you may have to get used to the idea of using higher pedal pressures and leaving longer braking distances—'just in case'.

The problem of reduced acceleration can be frustrating at times when you want to get past slow-moving trucks and buses, but for your first few miles at least you won't be in a tearing hurry. Provided the van isn't too heavy for the car, performance shouldn't drop off too much.

Don't forget the extra 15 feet or whatever behind you—especially when overtaking. That may sound silly, but it's all too easy for the novice caravanner to cut in early after overtaking and to clip the vehicle behind, or, worse still, to knock an unsuspecting cyclist from his bike. Pedal cyclists in particular are a danger to look out for because they are often a little unsteady at their slow speed—make sure you give them a wide berth.

Whenever you take to the road, as when driving the car alone, you should be as aware of the traffic behind you as of that in front. When you are caravanning, this rule is doubly important; and there is the added problem that it's not always so easy to get the correct view. If you are in the least bit dissatisfied with your view to the rear, you should find out what sort of mirror or periscope system will give you the clearest view and then buy it.

Some caravanners give caravanning a bad name because they cause traffic congestion. There is categorically no need for this situation to arise *if* you behave sensibly. A modern caravan outfit that is well matched can be virtually as lively and as manoeuvrable as a solo car. With the proper outfit and the 50 mph speed limit there is no need for you to hold up traffic provided you drive considerately.

Though one caravan outfit is normally a pretty easy obstacle for a driver to overtake, two outfits close together may prove impossible. Never, ever drive in convoy with another caravan, even if the other family are your best friends and you are heading for the same site; arrange to meet each other at a pre-determined point an hour's drive away if you wish, but having decided on that meeting point you should go your separate ways.

The second golden rule is to keep an eye on what's going on behind. There may be occasions, on gradients for example, where you cannot avoid moving more slowly than the rest of the traffic. Keep an eye on your rear-view mirror and if you collect a 'tail' of more than six cars, pull into the first lay-by and let them all pass. It is only common sense and common courtesy.

Whenever you stop on a slope, apply the car handbrake firmly. Don't rely on your footbrake alone (apart from anything else you'll just make your leg ache) and don't hold the outfit still by slipping the clutch if you are on an upward slope. This is bad enough practice in a solo car, but with the added weight of the caravan you're just asking for a burnt-out clutch.

Practise things like hill starts and reversing on a quiet Sunday morning in an area where there will be little traffic. Should the occasion arise where you do find it impossible to get away on a hill, first reduce the load by asking all your passengers to get out of the car and walk up. They can even give a push (on the back of the car, *not* the back of the van) to get you started. If you still find things a little tricky, take off at an angle across the hill rather than straight up it — but have someone posted at the top of the hill to make sure there's no one coming the other way! Of course, you should never tow a caravan so heavy that you get in this position anyway.

Reversing a trailer is an art, but once you have got the hang of it, it becomes automatic. The important thing to remember is that a trailer moves in the opposite way to its tow car; reversing a car with the steering wheel moved to the left means the back end of the car goes left too — but the back end of the trailer goes *right*. The procedure is explained more fully in Chapter 6.

Overtaking is something that demands extra special care, and bicycles are a particular hazard. Never cut in too early after overtaking

Chapter 6
Towing

If money was unlimited, it would be best to buy a new car *and* caravan together; then you would have no excuse for not making the perfect combination. Unfortunately not many of us are in that position and if we are paying out a lot of cash for a caravan, we have to make do with whatever car we already have.

Basically it's true to say that any modern car is capable of towing a caravan of some sort, but with a caravan in tow you must make doubly sure that your car is in good, reliable condition before you set out. Towing obviously puts extra strain on many parts of the car but you should ensure

particularly that the brakes, clutch and suspension are in good working order.

You will of course need a towing bracket fitted to the rear of your car, and an electric socket to feed power from your car's lighting system to the caravan's lighting circuit, so that the lights on both vehicles work in unison. Can you fit these items yourself?

Fitting the towing bracket

Proprietary towing brackets come with mounting instructions, but their fitting nearly always entails the removal of bumper bars and other items and drilling holes through body/chassis members. It's a job most handymen can tackle if they're armed with a good set of spanners, some penetrating oil, possibly an electric drill and certainly a fair amount of patience — undoing badly rusted bolts can be time-consuming and annoying.

If you do intend to fit your own towing bracket, make sure that you can get the rear end of the car well up off the ground (supporting it on axle stands or ramps) so that you can work clearly, and that the car has some secondary means of support — just in case. If you don't have the necessary tools, you can hire them; you could, however, find yourself paying more in hire fees than a garage would charge to fit the bracket. If you take your car to a garage or towing equipment specialist, it shouldn't take a fitter more than one or two hours to fit a towing bracket to a modern car.

You will have to buy the bracket itself (the price depends on its construction and on the type of car you have). On top of this will be the cost of the towing ball.

Wiring the electrics

The internationally agreed system for wiring up the caravan electric socket uses a seven-pin arrangement that takes leads from the following points in the car wiring set-up: left-hand and right-hand side lights, left-hand and right-hand indicators, stop lights, earth and a spare live wire for electrical equipment installed in the van.

It is usual to attach the seven-pin socket to the towing bracket using a mounting plate fitted behind the towing ball. A seven-core cable passes from the socket into the car boot, where the seven individual wires are joined into the car's wiring loom at a convenient point — at one of the rear light units, for instance.

A special plastic seven-pin socket for use when additional electrical equipment is fitted to the caravan

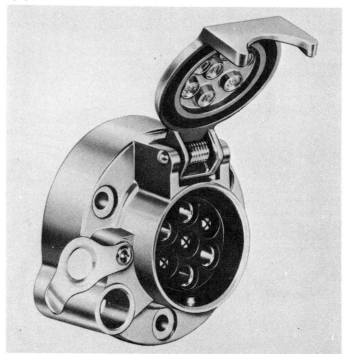

Again this is a job you can tackle yourself, and if you buy a kit of parts, instructions are usually supplied. But if car electrics are a mystery to you, it's better to pay an expert a few pounds to do the job for you. If you do attempt the job yourself, remember to disconnect the battery before tampering with the car's lighting circuit.

As I mentioned briefly in the last paragraph, if you want to save the bother of buying all the parts separately, you can buy a trailer wiring kit from any one of a number of firms. This should contain the socket, mounting plate, connectors and wire, and one other important item — a heavy-duty flasher unit. You won't get a seven-pin plug to go with your socket because there will be one fitted to the caravan. The heavy-duty flasher unit replaces the one that normally works your car indicator lights or, in some cases, forms an addition to it. The standard type might not be powerful enough to cope with the caravan flashers too (it might produce an illegally slow rate of flashing), so you must boost its capacity by fitting the replacement or additional flasher unit.

An additional warning light has to be wired into your car dashboard too, so that any irregularity in the working of the caravan indicators can be spotted immediately from the driving seat.

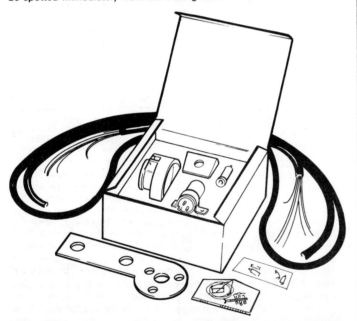

If you want to wire up your own tow car's electric socket, you can buy a kit of parts, like the one shown here. It contains a heavy-duty flasher unit, seven-core cable, seven-pin socket, mounting plate, dashboard warning light, warning light mounting plate, connectors and full instructions. Be sure to buy a kit that contains the right flasher unit for your car

The internationally agreed seven-pin system operates all the trailer's lights from the car circuit, leaving one live terminal spare for electrical equipment inside the van

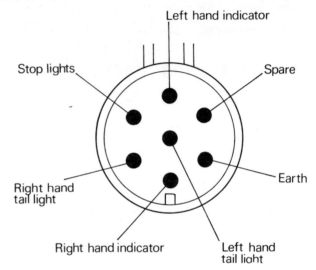

Matching car and caravan

Each car manufacturer lays down a maximum safe towing limit for each of his models; this is a rough guideline only, some makers being notoriously optimistic, while others give pessimistic weights. If you can't find the appropriate weight limit for your car in the handbook or from your local dealer, you should be safe if you bear in mind that the caravan's weight should not exceed three-quarters of the car's weight. This ratio is a rule of thumb only and has no legal significance.

The towing capacity of your car will also depend on its engine size and the engine's characteristics. Another rule of thumb often quoted is that the car will tow 1 hundredweight of caravan for every 100 cc engine capacity, but here again engine characteristics can make all the difference between a good tow car and a bad one. This rule also comes badly unstuck in the case of high-powered cars that weigh little but have large-capacity engines.

The most important thing to consider in assessing an engine's suitability for towing is not its power output (usually expressed in brake-horsepower) but its maximum torque output (in pounds-feet) and the engine speed at which that is produced. The higher the maximum torque output, and the lower the engine speed at which it's produced, the better. To quote an example, a car producing 100 lb.ft torque at 3,000 rpm is better for towing than one producing 100 lb.ft at 4,000 rpm; but the latter car is better than one producing only 80 lb.ft at 4,000 rpm.

You'll need to make full use of the engine's turning effort when getting your outfit away from a stationary position, and for this reason a car with four forward gears is better than one with three. And what about automatic transmission for towing? As a rule it's fine. Most automatics incorporate a 'torque convertor' and in practice this brings the bonus of maximum torque on take-off. The only point you have to bear in mind is that some car manufacturers recommend the fitting of a transmission oil cooler if you are going to tow with an automatic, and this means additional outlay unless the cooler is a standard fitting. Again this is a point to check with your dealer or handbook.

When you set about narrowing your choice of caravan, there is one other aspect of the car you must bear in mind: its kerbside weight. This is the weight of the car as supplied by the manufacturer, with oil, petrol and water and with the towing bracket fitted, but with no passengers or luggage inside. The caravan you buy will have a 'maximum gross weight' above which it cannot legally (or safely) be loaded, and it is important that this weight should be lower than the kerbside weight of the car; if it isn't you'll be restricted to a maximum speed of 40 mph instead of 50 mph when you take to the road in Britain.

If you intend to tow at 50 mph (and your outfit is legally qualified to do so) the kerbside weight of the car and maximum gross weight of the caravan must be prominently displayed on the respective vehicles and the rear of the tourer must carry a '50' plate similar to the familiar GB plate — but these points are more fully explained in Chapter 7.

Before you set off you may be worried about having a clear view to the rear of your van — as indeed you should be. The law says you must be able to see clearly to each side of the caravan's back end, and the most obvious way of ensuring this is to fit the tow car with additional or replacement wing mirrors with a wide enough field of view. There are various types of towing mirror on the market, from wing mirrors with extending arms to clip-on extensions for the standard, non-towing mirror.

There are also additional wide-view mirrors that attach temporarily to the car door or window, plus two completely different items: the roof-mounted car periscope, and — a new idea — a refracting disc that you stick

With the car and caravan outfit shown in the top drawing the windows are at such a level that the driver has a 'view through'. By looking in the car's internal rear view mirror, he can see traffic behind the caravan. (This should not of course stop him fitting external towing mirrors to the car.) The windows in the caravan in the lower drawing are too high to give the driver a view through, so he uses a roof-mounted periscope device on the car

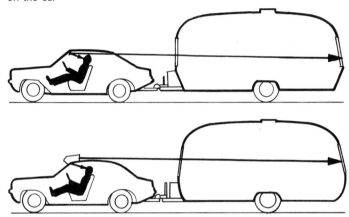

on the caravan's rear window and view via the car's internal driving mirror. The prism-section of the refracting disc gives a broad view of what's going on to the rear of the van and overcomes the dangerous blind spot of that area close to the van and below its rear window. With a periscope you look through the car windscreen at the periscope's lower end, while the top reflects light taken through the caravan's front and rear windows. Periscopes are quite successful where the particular car/caravan outfit gives no through view — that is, you cannot see *through* the van using the car's interior mirror because the van's windows are too high or because the furniture inside obstructs the view.

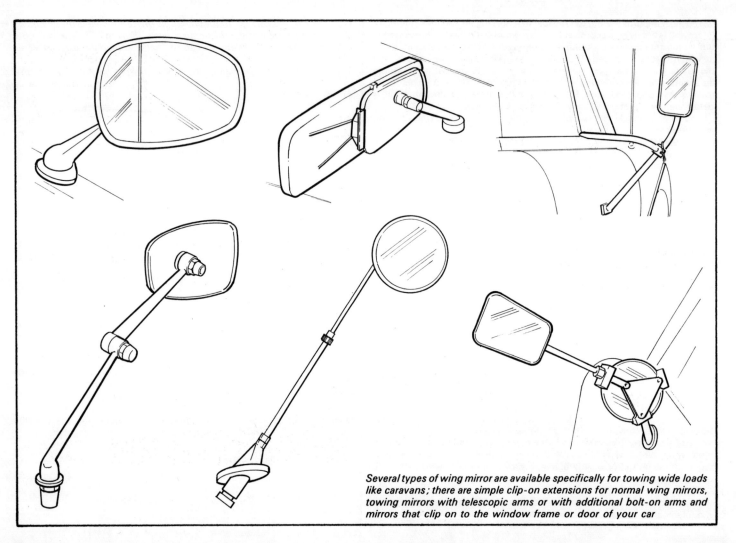

Several types of wing mirror are available specifically for towing wide loads like caravans; there are simple clip-on extensions for normal wing mirrors, towing mirrors with telescopic arms or with additional bolt-on arms and mirrors that clip on to the window frame or door of your car

Roof-mounted periscope

Clip-on door mirror

Towing troubles

We've all heard of caravans that sway from one side of the road to the other. This is very rarely because the caravan is badly designed or constructed; but it is almost always because the caravanner has put little or no thought into his choice of outfit and/or has badly prepared it for the road. Basically there are two types of bad caravan behaviour commonly experienced — pitching and snaking.

Snaking

Snaking — the violent, progressive swinging from side to side of the caravan's rear — is more dangerous and certainly more alarming. In almost all cases it can be cured by reloading the van with more weight towards the front. Don't, however, put too much weight at the front of the trailer (the heaviest items should be stored as near as possible over the axle line), but make sure the caravan noseweight — that's the downward weight at the coupling — is somewhere in the region of 1 hundredweight. It certainly shouldn't be less than 90 pounds, and rarely can it safely go above 150 pounds when the van is stationary; if you have too high a noseweight, the van will be difficult to handle and, what is more important, you may

damage the car's suspension. Another help in really bad cases of snaking is to fit some kind of stabilizer — usually some sort of friction-damped coupling between the car and caravan — but stabilizers are not widely used.

If despite this advice you should ever experience snaking, keep calm, grip the car's steering wheel tightly and decrease your speed *very, very* slowly until you reach a speed at which things return to normal. The worst possible thing you can do is to brake, as this will accentuate the caravan's pendulum effect on the car. If you understand the theory of snaking, you may think that hard acceleration would pull the caravan into line; this sounds fine in theory, but you will find your tow car doesn't have enough power to jerk the caravan back into a straight line.

Pitching

Pitching is a less dangerous but nevertheless tiresome effect, where the front end of the caravan 'nods' up and down — which in turn of course rocks the back of the car. The causes of pitching are too high a noseweight or, more probably, weak rear suspension at the back of the car. If your tow car is more than three or four years old, the rear springs have probably become 'tired', but even with a new car you may find the rear suspension less strong than you would like, particularly if the car has a long tail overhang.

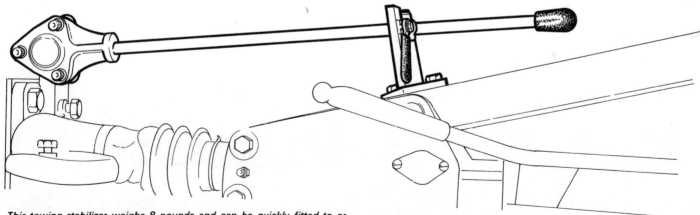

This towing stabilizer weighs 8 pounds and can be quickly fitted to or detached from the car and caravan

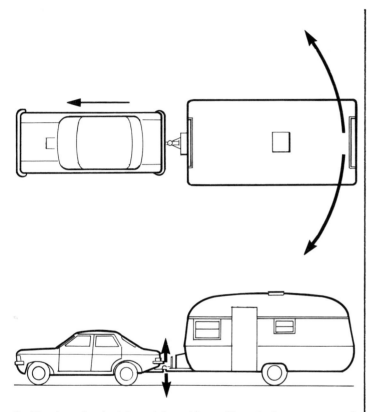

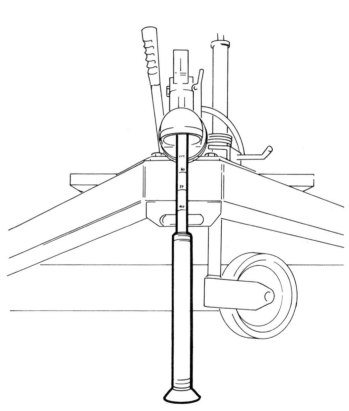

Snaking (top drawing) is a violent side-to-side swinging movement of the caravan, usually due to incorrect loading. Heavy items should be stored over the van's axle, not at the rear, and the downward force at the coupling should be around 1 hundredweight when stationary. You can measure this weight approximately by standing the caravan jockey wheel on the bathroom scales. Pitching (lower drawing) is an up-and-down movement at the front of the caravan caused again by incorrect loading or by the car's suspension being too weak. Cure the problem by redistributing the van's contents, or by boosting the car suspension with suspension aids

Having the correct noseweight plays an important part in maintaining stability when towing. The special noseweight balance gives a direct reading of the static download at the caravan's coupling.

Right

Wrong

Wrong

Viewed from the side, your caravan should ride level with its tow car—or very slightly nose-down. If the front end is more than a couple of inches lower than the back, you should check the noseweight and, if necessary, boost the car's rear suspension. If your van rides nose-up, even with the correct noseweight, it may be necessary to lower the car's towing ball to correct the alignment; use a 'drop plate', available from your towing bracket supplier

The remedy for too high a noseweight is, as has been said, to transfer weight within the caravan to somewhere over the axle line (not to the back of the van), and the remedy for sloppy back-end suspension is to boost the capacity of the car's rear springs. This can be done with 'suspension aids', which come in a variety of guises suitable for different types of suspension. The type of suspension aid you will be able to fit will depend on the system used for your car suspension, and on whether or not you want it quickly readjustable for those times when you are not towing. Some suspension aids can be fitted quite easily by the home handyman while others are best left to a competent garage. Consult the supplier on this point.

If you are in the market for a new car, it is worth remembering that cars with long tail overhangs are more prone to pitching because the noseweight acting at the very end of the car has a greater leverage effect. Also, cars with a 'solid' rear axle tend to tow better than those with fully independent suspension.

Many of you with front-wheel drive cars may be worried about this system's suitability for towing. Generally speaking front-wheel drive cars are surprisingly good, and it's only when you get the combination of a high noseweight and perhaps a slippery surface (maybe wet grass) or a slope that the front wheels tend to spin. In all normal conditions front-wheel drive is fine, and many such cars—for example the British Leyland 1800/2200 range and Citroen's GS—are superb tow cars.

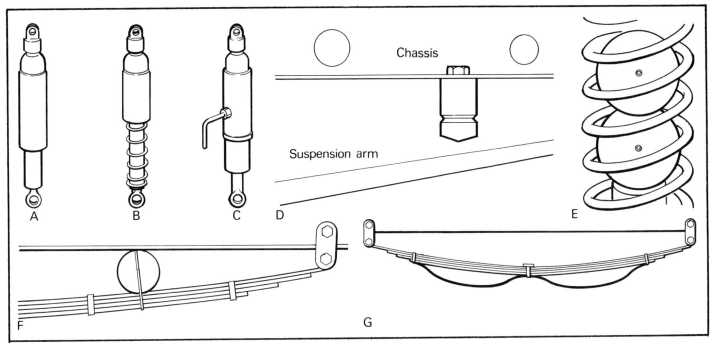

Chassis

Suspension arm

A B C D E

F G

Seven types of suspension aid:

A – replacement shock absorber. *To bring your car's rear suspension back up to scratch for towing all you may need is replacement shock absorbers. The best types are considerably stronger than those usually fitted during the car's manufacture, and some are adjustable for wear and ride*

B – shock absorber with spring. *This type of suspension aid uses a tough replacement shock absorber fitted inside a progressively rated coil spring. The effect of the spring becomes greater as the shock absorber is compressed further*

C – air-filled shock absorber. *This shock absorber has a top chamber that is filled with air. Lines are taken from the units to convenient points on the car body and you just 'top them up' before towing, in the same way that you might adjust your tyre pressures*

D – replacement bump stop. *This simple hollow rubber device replaces the normal bump stop at your car suspension's point of furthest travel. Instead of reaching a full stop, the suspension arm contacts the hollow rubber unit and gradually compresses it*

E – coil spring inserts. *Useful for cars with coil spring and torsion bar suspension, these hollow spheres are inflated to a few pounds' pressure and give strength to the normal suspension as they are squashed. Some types are ready inflated, others are fitted with valves for easy insertion*

F – clamp-on hollow sphere. *Similar to type E, this hollow sphere can be clamped on to a leaf spring between the spring and the car body or chassis*

G – add-on leaf spring. *Again designed to help leaf spring suspension, this aid is really just an additional leaf that clamps on to the original set-up. It is bow shaped for extra strength*

How to reverse

As I have said before, reversing a caravan needs patience and a certain knack that comes with experience. The first thing you have to consider before moving your outfit in reverse, however, is whether or not the caravan brakes will come on—after all, overrun brakes work by pushing back the coupling head.

Many of the latest caravans are fitted with special brakes that automatically lock out when the wheels are turning backwards, but with others you have to take steps to stop the brakes coming on. You do this by holding back a lever (known as the reversing stop) on the coupling. Go to the coupling and push the lever back until it clicks—you may have to exert pressure to push the caravan away from the car to get the brakes right off. When the reversing stop has clicked into place, you can get back into the driving seat and manoeuvre the outfit backwards without fear of the caravan brakes coming on. As soon as you drive forwards again, the revers-

ing stop will revert to its original position and the overrun brakes will work again; this is a safety requirement, but it does mean that if you don't complete your manoeuvre in one go you must get out of the car each time to reset the catch before you reverse. There are electric conversions for reversing stop mechanisms if you fancy the idea.

Reverse your outfit slowly, remembering if you are turning that as the rear of the car goes one way, the rear of the caravan will go in the opposite direction. Also, the length of the van exaggerates the amount of movement, so only a slight turn of the steering wheel will make the van swing out a long way. If you are going round a corner, back the van round remembering these rules, and then follow on with the steering wheel turned the other way to get the car round.

Before reversing your caravan outfit at all, have someone stationed at the back to make sure your path is clear and, if necessary, to give you guidance.

Reversing a caravan requires a lot of practice. Remember that as the back end of the car goes one way, the back of the caravan will move in the opposite direction. Once you have guided the caravan round the corner, you must apply the opposite lock to manoeuvre the car round

Chapter 7
Safety and the law

Compared with other road-going vehicles that are self-propelled, the caravan is an uncomplicated unit. There is little in it to go wrong, it doesn't carry passengers on the road and, provided you are sensible, you are unlikely to come to harm in it or to have trouble in satisfying the law's demands.

From the standpoint of safety we must consider caravans from two different angles — as moving vehicles that use our highways and as stationary, temporary homes on site; for convenience I will deal with them in that order.

Preparation for the road

Before you consider taking your van out on the road there are one or two points to watch. First, are the tyres properly inflated? If the van has been standing for a long time, some loss of pressure can be expected. It's important to make sure the correct inflation level is maintained — the pressure required should be stated in the caravan's handbook if one is supplied, but otherwise your dealer or the manufacturer should be able to advise you. In the last resort you can write to the chassis manufacturer, quoting the make and model of your caravan, or indeed to the tyre manufacturer. Most caravans use a tyre pressure of around 30 psi.

If the tyre pressures are all right and the tyres are in good serviceable condition, the next thing to check is that the brake-actuating mechanism is working correctly; push back the coupling and make sure that the brakes

come on and are properly adjusted (see Chapter 10).

Back your car up to the caravan ready to hitch up and then, making sure the caravan handbrake is fully applied, wind up the corner legs if they have been down. Lift the coupling head (either manually or by winding down the jockey-wheel stem), release the handbrake and guide the coupling on to the towing ball. Unlock the jockey-wheel stem and pull back the safety catch on the coupling head, and the ball and socket should engage firmly. When you release the safety lock, you should not be able to pull the coupling head off the towing ball. Raise the jockey wheel fully and tighten the locking screw on the stem so that it cannot fall down during the course of your journey.

Some caravans are fitted with a safety chain; if yours isn't and it would add to your peace of mind, then buy one at any caravan accessory shop. The idea of the safety chain is not to keep the car and van together in the extremely unlikely event of the coupling breaking. The point is that the chain — which passes over the towing ball or, in some cases, fits on to hooks specially provided on each side of the ball — is designed to pull the trailer brakes on and then snap. For this reason you shouldn't fit a heavier gauge safety chain than the one that's provided, in the misguided hope of making your outfit safer.

If all this talk of safety chains makes you think there is a possibility of your car and caravan coming adrift on the road, let me put your mind at rest. It is so rare an occurrence these days that the idea can just about be discounted in normal everyday motoring.

Finally, before driving off you must plug in your electric socket and check that all the lights are working — and do check *all* the lights. Even if you intend driving only during the daytime, you may run into fog and need your tail lights. Check with the help of a friend that the sidelights, brake lights and indicators are all working, trying each function separately and then all together, just to make doubly certain there are no faults.

Having made sure that your mirrors are adjusted correctly and that the road ahead and behind is clear, you may drive off with confidence.

On-site safety

Once you have reached your site, uncoupling the outfit is a reversal of the above procedure: unplug the electrics, drop the jockey wheel and lock it, release the coupling lock, lift off the coupling head and apply the caravan handbrake. If you are on any slope at all, it's wise to put chocks behind the caravan wheels.

You'll want to set your van level on site and you can do this by winding down the corner legs with the jack handle provided. If there's a big height

difference to make up between one side of the van and the other, or between ends, you may need to place something under one or two of the legs; use flat pieces of wood or brick, or something else that won't give way.

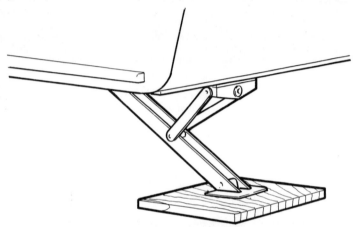

Your caravan will be fitted with wind-down legs at each corner. These are designed to help level the van on site. On very rough ground you may find you need to put packing pieces under one or more legs, and on soft ground flat pieces of wood will help disperse the load. Don't use the corner legs to jack up the caravan when changing a wheel

Fires in caravans are pretty frightening occurrences, though thankfully they don't happen very often. The most dangerous aspects of caravan fires are the speed with which they spread and the limited escape route for families trapped inside. A fire can result from fat catching fire at the cooker, from careless use of matches when dealing with gas appliances or simply from a cigarette end inadvertently left on a table top. All these things can be avoided with a little forethought, so make sure everyone in the caravan — especially children — are made aware of the dangers and are familiar with basic firefighting procedures.

The most important thing when a fire occurs is to save life. If a fire starts, however small it may be, your first consideration must be to get everyone out as fast as possible — no going back for transistor radios or expensive cameras. You should always keep a fire blanket and a fire ext-

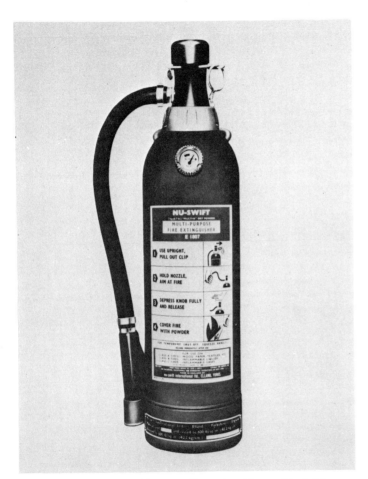

For safety's sake you should carry a fire extinguisher or blanket in your van — and make sure every member of your family knows how to use it. Fire extinguishers should be of a type that will deal with LP gas fires as well as normal domestic and electrical fires

When your gas cylinder is empty and you have to change the regulator, do so in the open air. It should not need stressing that there should be no naked flames about

inguisher inside your caravan and make sure every member of the family knows how to use it. Make sure your extinguisher is big enough for the job and can deal with a range of different types of blaze—including that of burning liquefied petroleum gas. Carry a large, cylinder-type extinguisher with British Standards approval. Never rely on an aerosol extinguisher in your caravan.

Bottles of liquefied petroleum (LP) gas may sound like potential bombs to you if you aren't used to them, but provided you follow a few simple rules you shouldn't come to any harm. The gas is stored in liquid form in pressurized containers. When you undo the valve on top the vapour escapes; one small drop of liquefied gas produces a vast amount of vapour.

The gas (most caravanners use butane—see Chapter 8) is heavier than air and thus collects near the floor if a leak occurs, so whenever you change cylinders or fit regulators make sure that you do so out in the open air or in a very well-ventilated area. And don't smoke when dealing with LP gas cylinders.

When you buy a full cylinder of gas it will be fitted with a plastic plug at the outlet. Don't remove this plug or disconnect any supposedly empty cylinder unless the valve on top is securely closed; an arrow on the valve wheel will tell you which way the closed position lies.

Whenever you fit a regulator to a gas bottle, ensure that the sealing washer is in good repair. If it appears even slightly worn, replace it—it will cost you only a few pence and may save a life. The washer and the flexible hose that takes gas from the cylinder to the input for the caravan cooking, lighting and other circuits is made from special materials that are impervious to LP gas—*not* rubber, which will allow gas to seep through. If the flexible hose attached to your caravan becomes worn, replace it only with LP gas hose bought from a specialist or caravan shop.

Always make sure there is plenty of ventilation when you use gas appliances inside your caravan because they use up oxygen from the atmosphere. Never leave a heater burning all night unless it draws its air for combustion from outside and passes its waste gases straight out through roof or wall flues, and always make sure last thing at night that all the other gas appliances are properly extinguished. If you have a gas fridge or flued heater and intend leaving it running all night, the gas must obviously be left on at the cylinder. In all other cases turn off the gas cylinder valve before you go to bed at night.

If you have the slightest suspicion of a gas leak in your caravan, get it attended to by an expert. If you must look for the leak yourself, do so only by rubbing soap solution on the suspect pipes or joints and watching for bubbles. *Never, ever* use a lighted match or other flame.

Almost invariably children enjoy caravan holidays and they can lend a hand with a number of jobs, from winding down the corner legs to helping erect the awning. Make sure, however, that they are taught the dangers of interfering with the coupling and the gas equipment

Caravans and the law

Generally speaking there are few laws laid down specifically with regard to caravans, or at least few with which you need to concern yourself. The law relating to caravan sites is dealt with more fully in Chapter 12, but as far as the trailer itself is concerned, the two main groups of laws you should be aware of concern towing and the construction of the caravan and its equipment.

First, the law does not restrict the *weight* of the trailer you can tow — though common sense will. There is nothing in law to stop a Mini owner towing a caravan weighing 2 tons, though of course he wouldn't get very far and he'd have even more of a job to stop. What the law does do is to lay down different speed limits for outfits that conform to certain requirements and those that do not.

The laws I shall quote refer only to ordinary cars towing caravans, and not to commercial vehicles or what are termed 'heavy motor cars', for which certain conditions do not apply.

If you want to tow your caravan at up to 50 mph on roads where this speed is permitted, then the caravan's maximum gross weight — that is the most it is allowed to weigh when fully loaded — must be less than the kerbside weight of your tow car. Also the weights relating to each vehicle must be prominently displayed on the left-hand or nearside of the respective vehicles. Both weights must be expressed in the same units, and if you use metric measures, the units must be kilograms.

You will also need a '50' sticker or metal plate on the back of your caravan. Specific sizes are laid down for the black circular or oval background and the white or silver figures, but since they are cheap you are unlikely to think of making up your own.

If your car and caravan outfit don't conform to these regulations in any way, or if you don't wish to carry the weight signs or '50' sign, you will be subject to the lower limit of 40 mph, even on motorways.

Caravan outfits are allowed on motorways, as no doubt you will have seen, but cars towing trailers of any sort are not allowed to use the outside lane on three-lane 'M' roads.

In Britain the maximum width for any caravan towed by an ordinary car is 7 feet 6 inches, and its maximum length is 23 feet (strictly speaking it is 7 metres but this is only a fraction less). These are points of only academic interest to you because no British caravan maker produces towing models outside these dimensions — for the home market anyway.

To a certain extent you can assume that any new caravan you buy will conform to the current construction and use regulations, but that's no reason why you shouldn't be aware of the lighting requirements.

The rear of the van must carry two red tail lights, two red stop lights, amber direction indicators and an illuminating light for the number plate — all of which must work in unison with those at the rear of the tow car. There must also be two triangular red reflex reflectors at the back of the van and, if its body length is over 5 metres, it must carry rectangular amber reflectors on each side

Your caravan must have two red rear lights, and if it extends more than 12 inches beyond the centres of the tow car's side lights, it must also have two white side lights (these are invariably fitted). There must be two red brake lights at the rear, a light (white) illuminating the number plate and two amber flashing indicators. These lights must work in unison with those on the rear of the tow car (this also of course means they must not replace those on the tow car). In the case of the direction indicators, the rate of flashing must be within the limits of 60–120 flashes per minute. The tow car must be fitted with some means (usually a second warning light) by which the driver can tell if a direction indicator light on the trailer has failed.

Two triangular red reflex reflectors must be fitted to the rear of the trailer. The triangles must have equal sides between 150 and 200 millimetres (about 6 to 7½ inches) in length, they must be at the same height from the ground and they must be within 16 inches of the outside of the caravan.

If your van is over 5 metres long (that's about 16 feet 5 inches) excluding the drawbar, it must also carry two amber reflectors on each side if it is to be used in the hours of darkness, but again these should already be fitted to any new van you buy.

Every trailer weighing over 2 hundredweight unladen (and that includes all caravans) must have an efficient braking system. The normal system used in caravans is the overrun type (see page 20) but there is nothing to stop you having an electric or hydraulic system fitted if you think it will improve performance; the only requirement then is that the trailer brakes should work automatically whenever the car footbrake is applied.

Your caravan must also have a proper handbrake that will hold the van still on a gradient of at least 1 : 6·25. This handbrake by law must be applied when the trailer is detached from its tow car.

The tyre regulations for cars also apply to caravans; the tyres must be in sound condition with at least 1 millimetre of tread, and they must be correctly inflated to a pressure within 10 per cent of the vehicle maker's recommended pressure. One law that doesn't apply to both vehicles, however, is that concerning lights on parked vehicles at night. Side and rear lights are required on all trailers parked on the highway after dark, regardless of the type of road.

As mentioned, caravans are not required to be fitted with safety glass windows (though these are sometimes available at extra cost) and this is one of the reasons why you are not allowed by law to carry passengers in your moving caravan.

Anyone with a full driving licence may take to the road with a caravan outfit, but learner drivers are prohibited. There are no upper or lower age limits and no special test, and caravans are not subject to any form of additional road tax.

Finally, you are allowed to paint your caravan any colour you wish— and there is no log book in which the colour or the owner's name and address are officially recorded.

Chapter 8
A Guide to equipment

The modern trailer caravan is almost completely equipped for immediate use when you buy it, though of course there are things you will need to supply before setting off on your first holiday – bottled gas and bedding, for instance. There is also a big market in what can be described as caravanning accessories, and that covers optional extras not only for the van but for the car you tow it with.

Bottled gas

Starting with the caravan, you will first want a source of bottled gas for cooking, and maybe for refrigeration, heating or lighting. The type of gas caravanners use is a petroleum by-product that is stored as a liquid in metal cylinders. There are two common forms of liquefied petroleum (LP) gas: butane and propane. Butane is more commonly used in Britain and is much more widely available; propane has the advantage of boiling at a much lower temperature and so it is used in Scandinavia, the United States and other countries where caravanners are likely to be out in sub-zero temperatures, when butane cylinders would appear to 'dry up'. Although you can get propane cylinders in Britain (from Calor Gas) there is not a very regular supply of 10-pound cylinders – the size most caravanners use – to their stockists, so you might have to order in advance.

For British conditions you are better off sticking to butane cylinders, which can be exchanged very easily, remembering that you can exchange a blue Calor Gas butane cylinder for a red propane one later if you intend winter caravanning in temperatures below freezing. (You will in that case have to change the pressure regulator because propane and butane equipment use different screw threads.)

The most popular gas cylinder used by caravanners in Britain is Calor Gas's Mk 10, which holds 10 pounds of liquefied gas. In 1974 the company launched a new cylinder, called Caravangas, aimed directly at the leisure market; the cylinder is aluminium, to save weight, and will hold 7 kilograms – over 15 pounds – of gas. It also has a clip-on regulator to ease the process of fitting a full cylinder when one becomes empty.

You will find that the gas-bottle carrier fitted to the drawbar of your caravan will take two Calor Mk10 cylinders side by side, so that when one is empty you can switch over to the second. Take the empty cylinder to any Calor Gas stockist and exchange it for a full one. If you ever give up caravanning, you should return the cylinder to a stockist, who may give you a refund.

The other big supplier of LP gas for the touring caravan industry in Britain is Camping Gaz, which sells butane only. Camping Gaz issues three different

To reduce the pressure of the LP gas in your cylinder, it must be fitted with a suitable regulator. Propane and butane are used at different pressures in caravans and the regulators use different threads to make them non-interchangeable

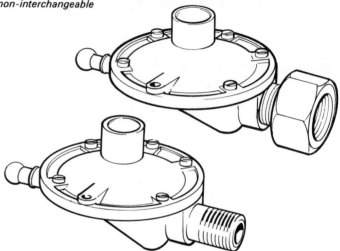

sizes of refillable container but the biggest holds only 6 pounds of gas and is the only one suitable for caravanning. Camping Gaz is available not only on a national network basis like Calor Gas but also throughout Europe, so if you take your caravan abroad you would be well advised to take at least one Camping Gaz cylinder even if you normally use Calor; don't rely on getting Calor Mk10 bottles refilled on the Continent. (It is hoped that Calor's Caravangas cylinders will be exchangeable with BP cylinders in Europe, but at the time of writing the extent of the European service network was not known.)

In Britain Calor Gas works out cheaper than Camping Gaz, principally because you have to buy it in larger quantities; also you *buy* Camping Gaz cylinders outright and there is no refund if you later give up using them.

With either gas, whenever you return an empty cylinder to the stockist it is sent back to the factory for checking and refilling, so you have no need to worry about the condition of the cylinder the stockist gives back to you. Some may look a little scruffy, but every full cylinder has been recently pressure-tested.

You will need a regulator for the gas cylinder and a flexible pipe that takes the gas supply into the caravan system, and this you can also get from the gas stockist. Each time you change cylinders you will have to remove the regulator with a spanner and refit it. Each time you do this you should check the condition of the washer at the join; replace it if there's any sign of wear.

If you are used to a gas cooker at home, it won't take you long to get accustomed to your caravan cooker—but if you use an electric cooker, you may be surprised to see how quickly things cook in the caravan. Be careful not to let things boil over—it not only causes a mess but can be dangerous in the confined space.

Fridges

Gas-operated caravan fridges are extremely economical to run and they are increasing in popularity. In fact many tourers now have fridges as standard equipment, and those that don't still have space for them. Some caravan fridges are made to run on 12-volt electricity, mains electricity *or* gas, or a combination of two of these, but the most common models are bottled gas only and vary in capacity from ¾ cubic foot to about 2 cubic feet. This may not sound much, but it's enough for milk, butter and a few other dairy foods (you'll find that with caravanning you can usually buy most foods along the way). Remember also that a full fridge operates more efficiently and economically than a half-empty one.

Different methods of igniting gas fridges are used, but there is usually either a flint mechanism or piezo-crystal; and once you have turned on the gas supply all you have to do is turn a knob or push a button.

Most instructions supplied with caravan fridges state that the fridge must be set exactly level to work properly. This is largely true, though in any case you will want to site your van as near level as possible for other reasons; but the fridge maker's advice does not mean that you cannot travel along with the unit working. Nearly all types will work quite well when subjected to the changing angles of a few degrees caused by the movement of the outfit on the road. Remember though that all naked flames must be extinguished if you stop for petrol.

You will see from Chapter 13 also that gas appliances of this sort must always be turned off when you board a cross-Channel ferry, so don't anticipate taking milk and butter from home for the first part of your continental trip; powdered milk and tinned butter are better if you are not sure of your supplies.

Small fridges hold more than one would think and can usually be fitted into existing storage units

Fitting a canvas awning to the side of your caravan will virtually double your living space on site

Awnings

Just about the most popular piece of optional equipment for touring caravans is the canvas side awning – and quite understandably so, as it virtually doubles your living space on site. If you look around the nearside edge of your van (the door side) you will almost certainly find that the manufacturer has fitted a section of channelling about $\frac{1}{2}$ inch wide all round. This is the awning channel, and the awning will be fitted with small runners that slide into and round the channel so that the caravan wall forms one side of the tent-like canvas enclosure. Awnings come in different shapes, sizes and colours, some having top, sides and front, while others have just top and sides or maybe even just a top sunshade.

Most models, however, are the fully enclosing sort, which owe a lot of their development to that of the modern frame tent; in fact many are made by firms specializing in the tent-camping market rather than in caravanning. The walls and roofs of such awnings are supported at the outer edges by a tubular frame of steel or anodized aluminium, and erection of the frame has been considerably eased in most modern designs by linking the major frame components with spring connections.

A folded awning, particularly if you have to pack it away wet, is a very heavy item to stow inside the caravan for your journey home or between sites, and to maintain stability it should not be placed too near the front or rear end of the van.

Bedding

Before you buy such luxuries as canvas awnings, you will need certain basic essentials for your first caravan trip – crockery, cutlery, a water carrier, waste-water bucket and bedding. Most of these you can take from home, though of course you should avoid the best silver and bone china! When it comes to bedding, experience has shown that the ideal solution is to provide a sleeping bag for each person. It's so much easier than having to make up conventional bedding with sheets and blankets each night, though of course you can use these materials from home if you prefer, or if you cannot afford bags in your early caravanning days.

Traditionally there are three sorts of filling for sleeping bags: down, kapok and man-made fibres. Down is best, but it is very expensive and in a caravan its biggest advantage – that it compresses to give a very small packed size – is less important than when camping. Sleeping bags filled with synthetic fibres are almost as thermally efficient; they are certainly far easier to wash and they are far less expensive. They don't fold down

A child's stretcher bed in position above a double bed

to a very small size, but there should be plenty of storage room for your family's sleeping bags in most tourers without encroaching on storage space not intended for bedding. Kapok bags are unsuccessful and best avoided, and are rarely found these days.

The most convenient types of sleeping bag have one continuous zip fastener all down one side and across the foot. If you open them right up, they can act as quilts on the beds at home. Two of these bags undone all the way round can be zipped together to form a double bag. But if you want to use a double bag in your caravan, it's better to buy a double bag in the first place; two single bags joined tend to be rather unwieldy and take up far more room than a purpose-made double bag.

Continental quilts — duvets — which have become very popular in Britain over the past few years, are quite suitable for use in caravans. But remember that they act with full efficiency only when their filling is sufficiently 'fluffed up' — and this means they should not be folded too tightly or stuffed into small bedding lockers when they aren't being used.

Store your bedding in the lockers provided under the caravan seating or in any other convenient locker, but remember that the cupboard you use should be ventilated to the interior of the van.

Here are a few tips on getting a good night's sleep in your van.

Many people have trouble in sleeping away from home, particularly for the first night or two, so make sure that when you go to bed you are relaxed and comfortable.

Don't break your home routine; if you are in the habit of having a cup of drinking chocolate or a sandwich before turning in, then do so on your caravan holiday.

Make sure you are warm when you get into bed. Remember that whether you use a sleeping bag, continental quilt or sheets and blankets, your bedclothes don't *produce* heat — they only insulate your body and keep in whatever warmth your body has at that time. Packing a hot-water bottle for your early or late holiday won't take up too much room — and you can even use a 12-volt electric blanket if you become that desperate!

Heaters

Keeping warm during the night is one thing, but daytime heating, particularly if you intend winter caravanning or visiting cold-climate countries, is another. Most inexpensive caravans are sold without heaters, but there is usually some provision for fitting them — sometimes a gas fire point is provided or you can have one fitted as an optional extra.

You'll find that caravan and camping accessory shops sell two types of heater: small, portable models and more expensive heaters that have to be fitted properly within the caravan. Unflued heaters are not ideal for use in touring caravans. If you do use one of these heaters, you should make sure that you always have plenty of ventilation by keeping at least a couple of windows open and by making sure that all vents fitted are unobstructed. Have the heater alight for only short periods at a time, and *under no circumstances* leave it running all night.

The only really safe answer to caravan heating is a model that draws its air for combustion from outside the van (this may be through the floor or side wall) and that passes the products of combustion directly out into the atmosphere again (through a side wall or roof vent). Heaters of this sort range from basic wall-fitting units to sophisticated central-heating systems with the heat relayed to small radiators fitted at strategic points around the van at floor level.

Many tourers are designed to take a flued heater at the base of the wardrobe unit. Sometimes, as I mentioned earlier, a gas tap is provided, and quite often there is an aluminium-lined recess. In these cases it is quite normal for the outlet flue to pass up through the wardrobe itself, usually with the pipe tucked into one corner so that it doesn't take up too much space. This is quite a safe arrangement, as this sort of heater normally reaches a very high level of efficiency and the flue gets only hand-hot. In fact it's an advantage for the small amount of heat radiated by the flue to pass into the wardrobe—it can do a useful job in drying out your clothes.

There is a third type of heater available, though so far as I know it is not fitted as standard equipment in any British caravan. This is the catalytic heater, and there are several makes on the accessory market. These heaters produce heat by a process that does not produce any flames—though a flame is needed at first to start the chemical action. Catalytic heaters are claimed to be safe for continuous operation.

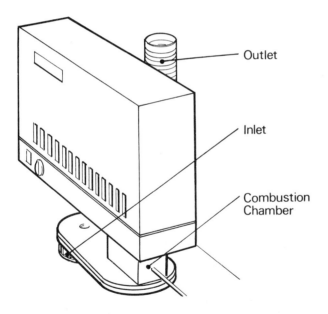

Outlet

Inlet

Combustion Chamber

A properly flued caravan heater draws its air for combustion from outside the van, has a sealed combustion chamber and passes the exhaust gases directly back into the atmosphere

A heater properly installed at the base of a wardrobe unit

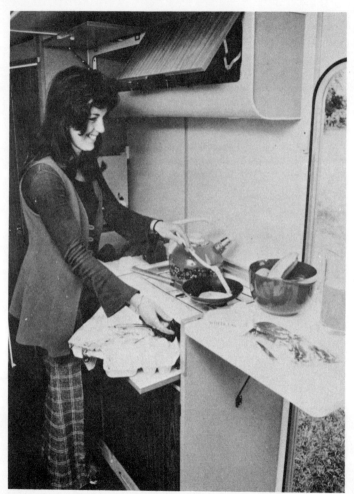

A standard cooking unit of grill and two burners with a fold-down working surface

Cookers

The majority of caravans are fitted with two-burner hotplates and grills as standard equipment, though small oven cookers are available on the accessory market and often feature on caravan manufacturers' option lists. Remember, though, that adding such extras eats into your weight allowance for personal items and also cuts down on your storage space. If a caravan manufacturer does not offer a fridge *and* an oven cooker as optional extras for a particular model, it is usually because of one or both of these considerations.

Water supplies

Only the most expensive British tourers are fitted with pressurized water systems that provide water to the sink at the turn of a tap, but you can go a long way towards easing the water-supply problem by fitting a water pump. The cheapest sorts operate manually by either hand or foot action; and fitting one of these is the sort of job any handyman can tackle. Foot pumps have the advantage of leaving both your hands free at the sink while you draw the water. Some types fit inside a locker and screw on to the floor; others fit through the floor and holes have to be cut; in this case make sure that those pipes or pump parts that are below the floor are carefully insulated before you try caravanning in cold weather.

If you want to go one stage further, you can fit one of several types of electric water pump, though of course you will need a supply of low-voltage electricity to power the unit; this can come through the spare terminal on your seven-pin car/caravan connection or from a second battery stored within the van. The second battery is a good idea if you have the money, space and weight capacity as it obviates the risk of running your car battery flat on site and gives you an additional power source for a host of other items from lighting to portable television.

The electric water pump can be fitted with a simple on/off switch, or you can fit a pressure switch that will cut in the pump whenever a house-type tap is opened. Installation in this case is a little more complicated, because the water system has to be made airtight.

One company manufactures a unit combining electric and foot-operated manual pumps, so that the foot pump can be used to pressurize the system first, or as an alternative should your power source fail.

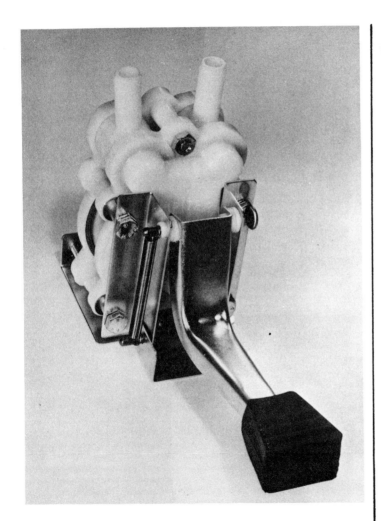

Lever-operated floor-mounted water pump

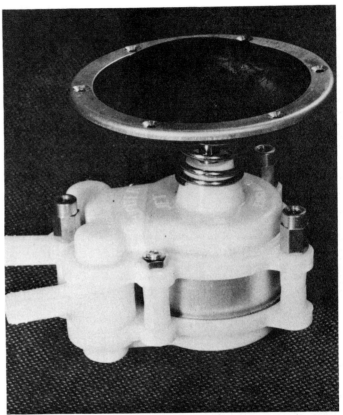

Water pump for underfloor fitting

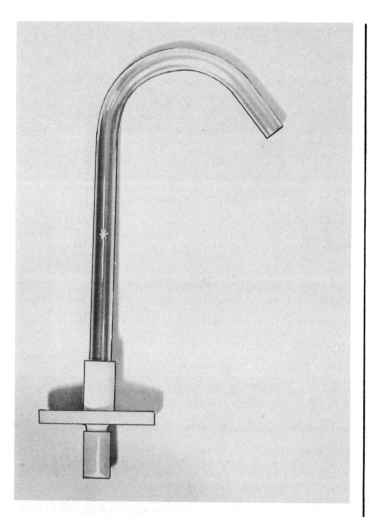

Typical spout for water outlet at the caravan sink

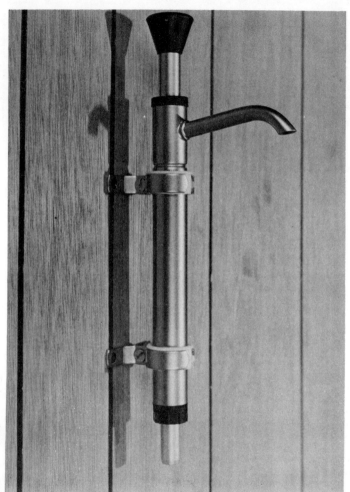

If you have no room elsewhere you can wall-mount a water pump of this sort

A spout like this will fold down into the sink when not in use

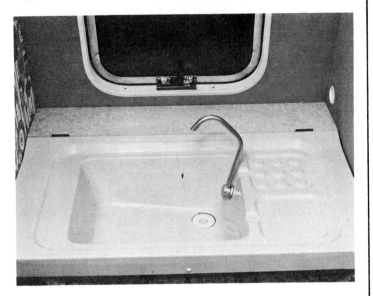

For many years caravans were fitted with gas lights, but in the recent past 12-volt fluorescent lighting has made big inroads. Most caravans sold in Britain today have both types

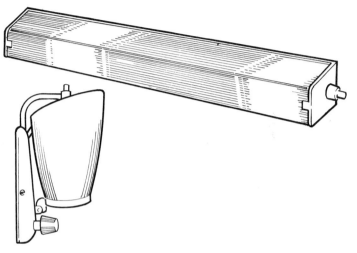

Lighting

Fluorescent lighting is one development that has affected caravan design tremendously over the last few years, since transistor circuit development has enabled manufacturers to turn out small units capable of 12-volt working. Two sizes are commonly used: the 8-watt tube and the 13-watt, measuring about 12 and 21 inches long respectively.

The light fittings are quite easy to install (full instructions are supplied), but you must be very careful to get the positive and negative leads round the right way – as indeed you must with any transistorized equipment. If you get the leads confused, the light either will not work or, in some cases, it may suffer irreparable damage.

Even caravans fitted with fluorescent interior lighting tend to have at least one gas lamp for stand-by use, so you'll have to get used to the idea of dealing with gas mantles. These are extremely delicate and, once fitted, should not be touched.

Second battery

With fittings such as electric lighting and water pumps within your caravan you may well begin to worry about the drain on your car's battery. The answer is to fit a second battery within the caravan. This should be an accumulator-type rechargeable battery (like your car battery) and ideally it should be stored in a ventilated locker somewhere near the centre of the van (where its weight will not matter so much when it comes to balancing the van).

To recharge the battery before or after your holiday you can use a normal mains/12-volt charger – the type you can get at any car-accessory shop. You may not be able to store enough power to last throughout your caravan holiday; the answer then is to recharge the battery as you go along by drawing current from the car's dynamo or alternator.

This is not quite as simple as it sounds because it means that an extra lead has to be connected between your car and caravan, and precautions

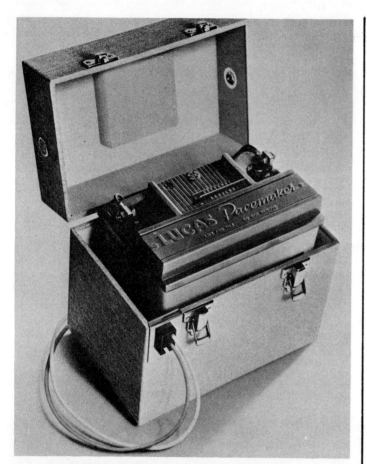

If you have several 12-volt electrical appliances in your caravan (e.g. lighting, water pump, television), it is a good investment to fit the caravan with its own car-type accumulator. This battery box has an external connection for the positive and negative leads

have to be taken to stop the car drawing current from the caravan when you start the engine. This is achieved by a piece of equipment called a blocking diode being wired in—something best left to a qualified motor electrician. If you want to go the whole hog, you can have your caravan fitted with a complete 12-volt distribution system with provision for recharging the caravan battery direct from the mains or from the tow car.

Mains electricity

Only a tiny minority of trailer caravans in Britain are wired for mains electricity and though such wiring can be added later, it is a very specialized job. Few caravan sites provide mains electricity hook-ups anyway, and on those continental sites where mains electricity is available, you'll find that the plugs and sockets, as well as the voltage, are different from those used in Britain.

Flyscreens

One useful accessory that can be fitted by the do-it-yourself caravanner is a flyscreen—invaluable if you are touring in areas where there are likely to be lots of mosquitoes or midges. The flyscreen is a very fine mesh panel that fits over window surrounds, doorways and roof-light openings so that you can let in the air without also letting in insects. Different styles of flyscreens are made by different companies, but the most popular types either clip on or fix on with Velcro fasteners.

Chapter 9
Sanitation

There are probably more popular misconceptions about chemical toilets than about any other aspect of caravanning, and the idea of using such things has probably put more people off caravanning before even giving it a try than anything else. The plain facts of the matter are that modern chemical toilets are convenient to use and to empty, they don't (or

Early on in your search for a caravan you will have to decide whether or not you want a model with a toilet room. Toilet compartments make ideal changing rooms or storage areas even if you start off with the idea of not carrying your own sanitation

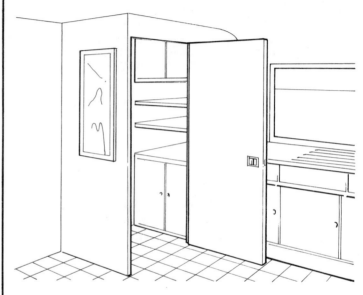

shouldn't) smell and in virtually all aspects they are as aesthetically pleasing to use as any form of household toilet.

When you buy a caravan you are faced with one definite decision: do you carry your own chemical toilet or do you rely solely on the facilities provided at the sites you use and the stops you make along the way? Many families start off with the idea that they will use only 'proper' facilities, but after one or two excursions with their caravan they soon come to realize that other more experienced caravanners deal with the sanitation problem in their own vans with barely a second thought. There is no embarrassment in going to the chemical toilet waste disposal unit to 'empty your tank' when everyone else is doing the same.

Toilet tents

If you set out with the intention of never carrying your own sanitation, you may have opted for a caravan without a toilet compartment. But if in the end you decide to have your own facilities, that need not deter you. You can buy a toilet tent. There are many makes available, in either canvas or nylon materials, but they all follow the same pattern in being upright, rectangular tents with just enough room inside for the chemical closet and its user. Pitch it just behind your tourer or in one corner of the awning if you are using one. If you prefer, you can buy an awning that already has a separate corner 'room' built in. Either way the arrangement is perfectly satisfactory — perhaps even better than having a toilet compartment as part of the van. The disadvantage is of course that you will have to find somewhere within the van to store your closet when you are travelling.

If your van does not have a toilet compartment – or even if it does – you can site your chemical toilet unobtrusively within a toilet tent pitched beside your van

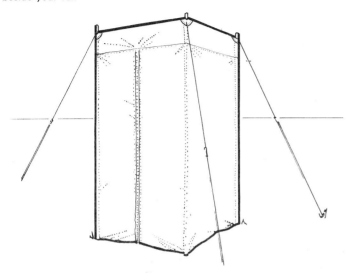

Chemical toilets

There are about half a dozen major manufacturers and suppliers of chemical toilets in Britain today; their products range from up-dated versions of the simplest 'bucket' type to sophisticated models with flushing mechanisms and pumps to empty the contents out into the disposal point. Each of the manufacturers recommends a particular brand of chemical to use with his product, but you'll find they all have the same three functions: to liquefy, deodorize and disinfect all waste matter. By the time you come to empty the toilet, the contents you pour out should be a germ-free, sweet-smelling liquid that is perfectly innocuous – provided you follow a few simple rules. Ensure that you add the right amount of chemical solution and water to start off with, and use only soft toilet tissue that can dissolve easily with the action of the chemicals.

Empty the contents of your toilet only into a proper chemical toilet disposal tip – you'll find these at many caravan sites in Britain – or, if you are on your way home, into your toilet at home. Don't be tempted to pour the contents into any old ditch or stream that takes your fancy, or into a septic tank, where the chemicals will cause harm.

Caravan toilets have undergone a mild revolution over the past few years, and though you can still get the conventional type with an outer casing (usually plastic these days), lid, seat and inner container, there has been a marked trend towards new, sleeker designs that have distinct upper and lower sections.

The top section is a plastic moulding fairly similar in design to a conventional domestic toilet, with a bowl, seat and lid. At the bottom of the bowl there is a flap that normally lies in the raised position. The bottom half of the unit comprises a holding tank, which you first partly fill with a solution of the chemical compound (powder or liquid) dissolved in water. After using the toilet, you activate some sort of lever or push button, which allows the flap to drop, emptying the waste matter into the holding tank, and gives a flush of deodorizing and sterilizing fluid. Some of these toilets are recirculatory, the same chemical solution going round and round again until the waste tank has been filled, while others have a separate tank for the chemical solution; this, once exhausted, has to be renewed at the same time you empty the holding tank.

In most cases the flushing mechanism is purely a mechanical action, but there are models available where this mechanism is electrically operated from your 12-volt supply. The majority of toilets of this sort have holding tanks that can be unclipped for emptying. Sometimes they are so designed that they can be carried suitcase-style to the nearest disposal point.

The most expensive types of chemical toilet are designed for permanent fixture in the caravan and are fitted with some means – manual or electric – of pumping out the waste matter directly into the disposal point. This is all very well in theory, but in practice it is rare to find a caravan site in Britain where you can drive the van up to the disposal point and simply flush away the toilet contents. The situation is very different in the United States, where this is the normal practice. American caravan sites *and* filling stations have 'dumping stations' where you can empty waste storage tanks. The situation in Britain might move along these lines, but meanwhile you can assume that you'll have to carry some sort of container to the disposal tip every day or two if you stay on a site without flushing toilets, or if you prefer to provide your own sanitation. By the way, don't expect to find chemical toilet waste disposal points on most continental sites.

Today's modern chemical toilets bear little resemblance to the original types many people still have in mind

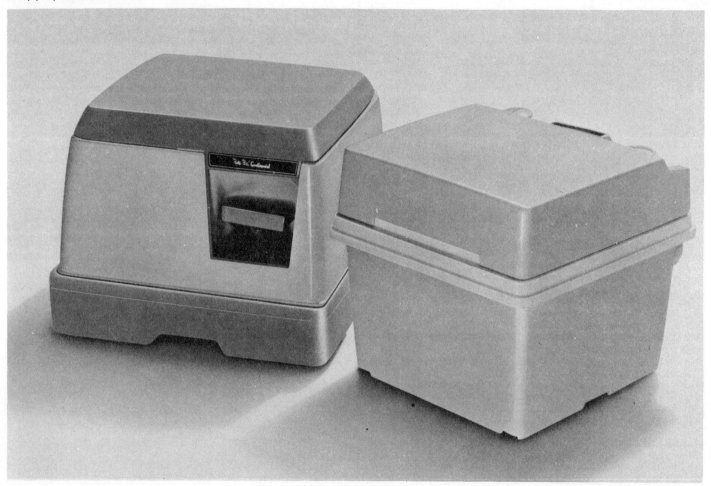

Site facilities

You will find that most site guides will indicate whether the site you choose has toilet facilities or whether you are required to provide your own. Most commercial sites in Britain, and virtually everywhere on the Continent, have proper toilet facilities, though on some foreign sites the arrangements may not be quite what you are used to. On the other hand, many sites established and run by clubs specifically for their members do not provide toilet blocks.

You will doubtless come across sites where the facilities are far from what you would like, but don't always blame the site operator. It is we, the public, who use the facilities and unfortunately some of us abuse them.

Disposing of used water

There are two other kinds of waste that caravanners on site generate — litter and water from the sink. It is possible to have a tourer fitted with a tank to collect the water used for washing and washing-up. But it will not collect toilet waste as well, because it is not permitted by law to store the two liquids in one central tank. Most caravanners, however, rely on the faithful plastic bucket set below the sink waste outlet under the caravan. There are special containers that slip under the caravan and can then be carried off to the waste-water drain; the advantage of these is that they hold more than a bucket and are easier to carry without spilling.

In any case, whatever you use, keep an eye on your waste-water container and empty it when the liquid gets within an inch or two of the top. You'll find that you become quite sparing with the amount of water you use in the caravan — it's amazing the difference it makes when you don't have water at the turn of a tap and when you know you might have a long trek to the tap when the supply runs out!

Forgetting to empty the waste bucket not only looks slovenly and untidy but shows thoughtlessness; if the bucket overflows and you leave a wet, soapy patch on the grass, you have spoilt someone else's chance of pitching their van there when you have gone.

Disposing of rubbish

You will soon learn to be tidy in your caravan (if you don't, you'll get swamped by the clothes, bedding, etc, left lying around). And to help to keep your van neat, you should maintain a central bin for rubbish. Small, swing-top kitchen bins are useful if you have the room to store one, but another sensible idea is to have a rubbish container tacked to the inside of one of the kitchen locker doors. You can buy units specially made for the purpose or improvise with plastic boxes.

If you smoke

Those of you who smoke will soon discover that caravans are rarely — if ever — fitted with ashtrays as part of their standard equipment. Don't forget to pack a couple when you leave home or, better still, fix a couple inside the van at strategic points — say, near the dinettes. If you don't, someone is bound to lay down a cigarette somewhere on a working surface or table top and cause a burn mark or worse.

A well-organised site

Chapter 10
Care and maintenance

Caring for and maintaining your caravan is easy—so easy in fact that a number of caravan owners neglect to carry out the small amount of regular maintenance required to keep their vans in tip-top condition; the result in many cases is a touring caravan that doesn't tow as well as it should, doesn't look as good as it should and is less comfortable to live in than it should be.

General cleaning

Your van will get dirty if it is left standing in the open air when you are not using it. On the road it will pick up traffic grime and thrown-up mud just like any other road vehicle. One way to prevent the front of your van taking too much mud off your car is to have the tow car fitted with a good set of rear mudflaps—it's surprising the difference they can make.

Stones thrown up against the front wall of the caravan form a more damaging hazard, and you may well find that the lower half of the van's front wall is made of a different material (hammered aluminium, for instance) that gives an added measure of protection. If this 'stoneguard' is not present, you may be able to improvise one yourself. Some caravan accessory shops sell stick-on types.

Having done your best to protect your tourer on the road, remember also that anything you can do to keep off rain, snow, bird droppings or whatever while the van is in storage will help to preserve its appearance. Though no full-size tourer will fit inside a normal home garage, if you store your van alongside the house you may be able to erect some sort of enlarged carport where the van will at least have a roof over its head.

Clean the outside of the caravan regularly with plain water, just as you would a car. Most of the aluminium sheeting used in today's caravan manufacture has a baked-on paint surface that is quite resistant and you should find a couple of hours' work with a hose, bucket and sponge well worth the effort. Wipe down the van with a chamois leather and give the windows an extra polish. Window frames are almost invariably anodized aluminium, which should need little or no attention and should not tarnish. You will need something substantial to stand on when you reach out across the roof and, of course, make doubly sure all the windows are closed before you turn on the hose!

In theory, then, the cold-water treatment is all the cleaning the caravan walls and roof should need, provided it is done regularly. If, like most of us, you neglect regular cleaning, some of the dirt may become more deeply ingrained and you'll have to tackle it with something stronger. Use one of the proprietary products for restoring colour to cars, but go very gently or you may go right through the paintwork.

Once you have the caravan in pristine condition, you can help to keep it that way by giving it a good coat of wax polish. There are no short cuts to a good wax finish, but it will make your task of cleaning it that much easier next time because most rain will simply run off. Don't forget that the caravan shell is aluminium and won't rust, so wet weather will not attack your van in the same way as it does your car.

Your caravan chassis is steel, of course, and many people ask whether some sort of undersealing should be applied. It can be, of course, though few people bother. If you want to give the undergear that added measure of protection, give it a good coating of bitumastic compound.

Tyres

Check the tyre pressures from time to time during the months when you aren't using the van and, of course, before every trip. It is unwise to let the van stand for months on end with the same area of tyre in contact with the ground, so move it a bit every few weeks just to rotate the tyres slightly. If the caravan will be standing in strong sunlight, it is best to drape something—sacking is ideal—over the tyres.

Brakes

Your new caravan will be supplied with a booklet issued by the chassis manufacturer that gives details of chassis lubrication, brake adjustment and relining. There are very few points that need greasing, and adjustment of the brakes, when needed, requires only a few turns of a buckle—check in the booklet how to tell when the brakes are properly set up, as different chassis makers use different brake systems. Brake relines are very rarely needed with caravans, but if you have tackled the job on a car you should be able to cope with it on your caravan.

If you have travelled a very great distance with your van, or if you have bought a second-hand model, you may find that the brakes tend to grab and appear to judder when you slow down the tow car. This is usually due to a worn damper in the coupling head overrun mechanism. The only

cure is to fit a new damper, available from caravan accessory shops or shock-absorber specialists. You will need to know details of the chassis make and type when you order the damper, and preferably the chassis number as well. Fitting the damper is not a very complicated task so long as you follow the instructions provided carefully. Do make sure you fit the damper the right way up.

Should you ever need to change a wheel on your caravan or get to the brake components, you will obviously need to raise the van. You can get special caravan jacks, but an alternative is to use a car-type scissor jack or hydraulic jack, picking up a suitable steel chassis member underneath. Make sure the handbrake is applied and that the other wheel is chocked on both sides before lifting one side of the van.

You may be tempted to raise one side of the caravan by putting down the corner legs on that side, possibly with packing pieces underneath. This is not what they are for, and it is something you should avoid unless you are really desperate, as it puts a strain on the whole structure.

The corner legs, whose proper purpose is to help to steady and level the van on site, should wind down quickly and easily by means of the handle provided. To help keep them free and clear of rust you should grease them at regular intervals.

Also make sure there is plenty of grease in the coupling head (and/or on the car's towing ball, where you should always remember to replace the cover when you are not towing).

Lighting

Check the caravan lighting every time you set out on a journey, and also in the winter months every few weeks – nothing is more infuriating than discovering at the last minute before setting off on your first summer break that some of the wiring has perished. Keep a set of spare bulbs for the front and rear lights, and also for the interior courtesy light if there is one.

It's a good idea to keep a couple of spare fluorescent tubes if your van uses these, though generally they last a long time and give plenty of warning before packing up altogether. Incidentally, if the unit in your caravan gives rise to interference on your transistor radio, try replacing the tube or moving the radio so that it faces another direction.

Battery care

If you have a spare battery in your caravan, take it out during the winter months and put it on a trickle charger from time to time – don't forget to leave it well ventilated when it's being charged. If it is a big car-type accumulator, swap it with your car battery for a while.

Gas system

Your caravan gas system should need little or no maintenance and should give years of trouble-free service. Leave it well alone unless you suspect a gas leak, when you should take it to a specialist who will carry out a pressure test with a water gauge. The only sort of leak detection you should try – and even then only if you have no alternative – is to rub soap solution on any suspect pipes or joints.

If the flame on your cooker jets is yellowy or if it tends to create soot on the base of your pots and pans, then suspect that the jets are letting too much air in. The jets can be adjusted and there may be instructions supplied with the van. If not, any gas fitter should be able to rectify the fault in a few minutes.

You'll find the air adjustment quite easily on any gas lamps in the van – it's a simple brass fitting on a screw thread that can be moved up and down the gas supply pipe to cover up or uncover a small hole. You will doubtless have to make some adjustment to these settings on the lamps when you use them the first time, but after that they should stay in adjustment provided you continue to use the same type of gas. If you switch from butane to propane, or vice versa, the flames on all your gas appliances may have to be adjusted to compensate for the different working pressure. Consult your dealer or a gas fitter on this point.

The gas cylinder itself and its regulator need no attention whatsoever and you shouldn't tamper with them. Under no circumstances should you attempt to dismantle an LP gas regulator; if you think it's faulty, you should return it at once to the nearest stockist who will send it back to the factory for testing.

Check the condition of your hose before using your caravan after the winter break because it might well have perished, especially if the van has been stored in the open air. If you can see any cracks in the hose when you bend it, replace it with proper LP gas hose from your caravan accessory shop.

Across the drawbar of your caravan you should find a gas-bottle carrier that will accommodate two Calor Gas Mk 10 cylinders or, as in this picture, two of the new Caravangas cylinders

Water carriers

Needless to say, when you aren't using your caravan you should empty its water tank or water carriers. Loose jerrycans should be stored upside down with the caps removed. You may find green algae forming in plastic water containers, but although it's said to be harmless, it is unsightly. You can get special preparations from the chemist to get rid of these stains, though I have heard that the powders you can buy for cleaning dentures work equally well.

It's not a bad idea to leave a window or two slightly open when the caravan is in storage, though of course you should not leave enough gap for water to get in or for any unauthorized person to gain access. Provided you remove all your personal equipment from the van, there won't be very much inside that any prospective thief could make off with—but that doesn't deter every crook. Quite often with such burglaries it is not what is stolen that matters so much as the damage and mess caused by the break-in—so don't leave an open invitation for the thief, even if your tourer is 'safely' stored at the side of your house.

Gas cylinders

For reasons of crime prevention if nothing else, you should not leave your gas cylinder(s) on the drawbar carrier when the caravan isn't in use. Take off each gas bottle and store it somewhere safe—a lockable garden shed or your car garage is ideal, but it's wisest to store the gas away from the house and away from the prying fingers of inquisitive children. The gas should always be kept well away from any heat source.

Awnings

If possible, store caravan awnings indoors where they are less likely to become damp. Although they should be kept somewhere dry, it is not a good idea to put them inside an airing cupboard or to use such a cupboard to get them dry in the first place. They should be allowed to dry out naturally before storage and should not be subjected to artificial heat.

Never leave your awning packed away wet for any longer than you can possibly help. If you do, mildew will form (you'll notice small grey spots appearing on the canvas) and eventually it will rot. As soon as the weather improves, erect the awning again and let it dry thoroughly before putting it away; feel along the seams, where there is at least a double thickness of cloth, to make sure the canvas is dry. If you are heading home and don't get the chance to erect your awning again, then spread it out in the garden to dry properly when you get home. Awnings are expensive items and are worth looking after.

If rust spots appear on a steel awning frame where the plating has worn away, rub down to the bare metal again with emery cloth and quickly paint over the affected area. If you break a spring link, you can buy a packet of replacement connections, complete with fitting tool, from camping and caravan shops.

Bedding

Sleeping bags don't require any special treatment, though opening them up and using them as quilts when you are at home serves the purpose of keeping the filling nice and fluffy, as well as doubling their usefulness. If you have been using washable sheet-type liners on your trips, the bags should remain clean for a long time, but when they do get grubby make sure you know exactly what filling they have before attempting to clean them. Those with fillings of man-made fibre are machine-washable (see the label for full instructions), but down-filled bags should be dealt with expertly by your local dry cleaners or laundry.

Take the mattresses out of your caravan and store them indoors for the winter months if you have room. If not, then take them out and give them a good airing at least a week or two before you next use the van; at other times store them on their sides so that the air can get to the sleeping surface and the undersides.

Chapter 11
Eating outdoors

You may be relieved or dismayed to find that most British caravans come equipped with only simple two-burner hotplates and a small grill. If you bought an American trailer, you would almost certainly find three boiling rings, a grill and an oven – but at the other end of the scale, if you bought a continental caravan you would probably get just two boiling rings alone. At least in British tourers there's somewhere to make the morning toast!

Today's rapidly developing convenience food industry is a boon to the caravanning cook who wants to prepare tasty meals in the quickest possible time. But remember that on a caravan holiday you are in the ideal situation to pick up really fresh fruit and vegetables along the way.

If you are going somewhere sunny, you'll probably find that you can do with just one cooked meal during the day, having cold meals at lunchtime. But what about the main evening meal, and when you are touring in not-so-hot climates? Chances are that you will want to eat out a few times to sample the local cuisine, particularly if you are in a foreign country. I always think half the fun of a holiday abroad is sampling the local food. Look out for inexpensive roadside eating places where the furniture and fittings may not be too grand but the food and the prices may be just what you want. In France watch out for the *Relais des Routiers* sign in café windows – always a good indication of good food at the right price.

If you can't afford more than a few meals in a restaurant, then at least try some local shopping for food. Take a look round one or two different food stores and it will soon be apparent what the local specialities are.

If you stay in Britain, you'll have more of an idea what to give the family and where to shop for the best buys, though of course you will have to get by without some things – home-made meat pies and cakes, for instance – unless your caravan is fitted with an oven cooker. Few low-price and medium-price caravans have ovens, but they are usually available as optional extras. But before you rush off and order one, think how many times you are likely to use it on an average two-week holiday. . . . I bet it doesn't amount to more than once or twice unless you're a really keen cook.

With a little forethought and planning, using pre-packed or partly cooked ingredients, you can prepare a delicious meal for the whole family using just two saucepans, saving both cooking and washing-up time. Tinned foods are still a good stand-by for caravanners. But because tinned

foods are heavy, they are best packed away low down in the caravan, in floor-level lockers rather than roof-level ones. And if the caravan is carrying a lot of weight, it should be concentrated as near as possible to the centre of the van.

Cooking utensils

There are several sets of non-stick cookware designed for caravanners and campers. Normally each set consists of three or four nesting pans with a smaller diameter than is normally used at home – ideally suited to caravan hotplates. Normally the largest pan at least is fitted with a lid that doubles as a small frying-pan.

China plates and crockery are best left at home. The best solution for caravanning is a good-quality set of melamine crockery. This isn't quite unbreakable – it's what the makers call 'break-resistant' – but it is a lot tougher than china and is quite pleasant to use. The better makes are not particularly cheap but they look better and last longer; in particular, they are much less likely to stain. Avoid using abrasives when washing up melamine crockery because this damages the surface and allows stains to form. You can buy special cleaning powder for the crockery, but if you wash up properly after each meal you shouldn't need to use it except now and then when the odd stain appears.

Foods to take with you

If you contemplate going abroad, it is best to find out in advance which of your essential or favourite foods are unavailable or much more expensive in the countries you are going to visit. Things that are normally worth taking with you if you are going abroad are tea, coffee, butter, tinned meats, biscuits and sweets. Butter is best bought in sealed tins, where it will keep without refrigeration until opened.

Drinking water

More important perhaps than food is drinking water – something we take for granted in Britain because none of us is ever far away from a piped supply. On the Continent things may well be different and you certainly shouldn't assume that the water available at taps or sinks round the site is drinkable unless it is so marked. If you have *any* doubts at all about your water supply, you must sterilize it before drinking. Water-purifying tablets are available from chemists' shops, or you can buy a sophisticated water-filtering unit to place somewhere in the supply pipe to your caravan sink. As a last resort you can boil the suspect water – but make sure the liquid is kept boiling vigorously for at least five minutes before you assume it is harmless.

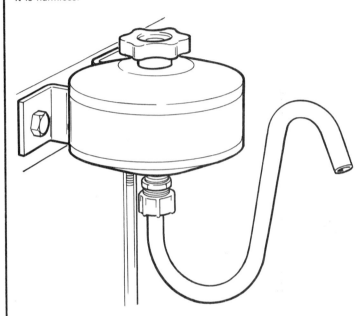

One of the most convenient ways of getting pure drinking water from a doubtful supply is to pass it through a purifying unit

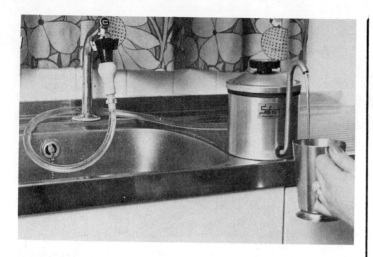

Fridges

Refrigerators are worth their weight in gold when you are caravanning in hot weather—and they are extremely economical to run. Powered by the van's LP gas cylinder, an average-size caravan fridge (1 or 2 cubic feet) takes only about as much gas as a single light fitting. But installing one can be expensive, so it's not something everyone can afford straight-away.

Insulated containers

A good alternative is the coolbox, which is an insulated container usually fitted with a lift-off lid.

Most types these days have plastic cases and simple wipe-clean interiors; between the exterior and interior layers there is foamed-in expanded polystyrene or polyurethane foam, which gives a very high degree of heat insulation. To go with the coolbox you can buy 'freezer bags'; these are soft plastic bags of special chemicals which, once frozen, help maintain a very low temperature within the coolbox. The idea is that you take the freezer bags to the site shop and get the proprietor to freeze them in his fridge before returning them to you. On many continental sites you will also find that ice is sold, either once a day from a travelling delivery man, or all day from the site shop. In an emergency a pack of frozen peas will do the job of a freezer bag.

Don't forget your vacuum flasks either—and remember that they are just as good at keeping food or drinks cool as they are at keeping them hot. If you have a fridge in your caravan, you can set off for a picnic with a container full of water, a bottle of squash and the vacuum flask full of ice cubes; this is a far better and more efficient method than taking cold drinks in the flask.

Barbecues

It is unfortunate in many ways, though many of you will appreciate the reasons of safety and practicality for it, that there are very few caravan sites left—in Britain at least—where you are allowed to set up an open fire. There is, however, one way of achieving almost the same result—and that is by using a barbecue. But always get permission from the site owner before lighting it.

Alternative types of water purifier

Chapter 12
Sites

Before considering the types of caravan site that are available in Britain and on the Continent, let me first answer the question of where you can stay with your caravan *outside* recognized sites. You must remember that even if a field or piece of heathland is utterly deserted and miles from anywhere, someone, somewhere, is the legal owner.

Farmland

If you want to avoid commercially run caravan sites and stay on open farmland, it is necessary for you to search out the farmer concerned and gain his permission. This is not only common sense and politeness; there is another side to the coin. A landowner may lawfully permit one caravan to stay on his land for one or two nights at a time, up to a total of twenty-eight days in any year. A farmer with 5 acres or more may permit up to three caravans on his land at any time provided the site is used for no more than twenty-eight days in any year.

Commonland

Open commonland often looks inviting for a quiet overnight stop, but here again you can land in trouble with the law. For a start, caravanning on many — if not most — commons is forbidden, and in any case it is an offence to drive a motor vehicle more than 15 yards off a highway.

Roadside verges

Land up to 15 yards away is still technically part of the highway, so though parking on roadside verges is not strictly an offence in itself, you could well cause an obstruction in the eyes of the law, and this might well bring about a prosecution.

Lay-bys

And what about spending the night in a lay-by? You may well have seen caravan outfits parking there overnight, particularly during the peak of the summer period in popular holiday areas. But even if you don't get prosecuted, you may well find a policeman at the door in the middle of the night telling you to move on.

Motorway service areas

The large parking areas at motorway service areas appear at first sight ideal places to stop for caravanners making long journeys, but there are usually signs forbidding the use of camping equipment (cookers, etc), if not overnight stopping itself. This is an unfortunate thing in many ways, and on the Continent the situation is often very different, but in Britain if you see a sign saying 'no caravanning' it is best to move on to a proper site.

Official caravan sites

Permanent, commercially run caravan sites are controlled in Britain by the Caravan Sites Act (1960). Anyone wishing to set up a caravan site in a particular area has to apply to the local council, which will — or will not, depending on circumstances — grant the appropriate licence. In doing so it is entitled to lay down specific requirements, such as the sanitation levels, number of fire extinguisher points, access routes and times of opening; some caravan sites are open all year and others only during the summer season, though the time during which caravanners use their vans is becoming longer as tourers become equipped with more and more home comforts.

Commercial sites such as these are run either by private individuals or by companies as money-making ventures, by local councils themselves or by clubs. Certain clubs are also allowed to run small sites, for up to five caravans at a time, without sophisticated facilities. These sites can be formed only when the club concerned has been granted a certificate of exemption, which in effect exempts them from the provisions of the Caravan Sites Act. Certificates are issued only to responsible clubs (such as the Caravan Club, Camping Club and Motor Caravanners' Club) whose members are entrusted to leave the site as they would wish to find it. These sites are usually on small areas of privately owned land with minimum facilities — a water supply, chemical toilet waste and rubbish disposal points. The sites are ideal for caravanners who are 'self-contained', and who are looking either for an overnight stop *en route* to their main destination or for an 'away from it all' site for a longer stay.

The other sort of site, which has a licence and therefore usually has more in the way of facilities, may vary from a rural location with only a water supply and basic toilets to a highly organized holiday-camp-type village with evening entertainment, made-up roads, swimming pool and restaurants. Somewhere between these two extremes every caravanner should be able to find a site to suit his particular taste.

Generally speaking, club sites and those run by local councils and bodies like the Forestry Commission have only toilets, washing and laundry facilities, plus in some cases a small shop selling groceries, gas supplies and other small items. Privately owned and run sites are more likely to be more highly developed because it is hard to make a caravan site pay solely on takings from overnight bookings.

Depending on the style of the site, you may be free to pitch your caravan where you like or you may be given a numbered area to use. If you are given a numbered area, stick to it; if free to pitch where you like, then be sensible and leave enough room between you and your neighbours so that they won't be bothered by your noise, your children or anything else.

There are still a lot of rural sites in Britain that give you a chance to get away from it all. This peaceful woodland setting is the Caravan Club's site at Fallowfield Dene, Acombe, Northumberland

Site charges

Charges vary quite considerably between sites, but they are liable to be highest in popular touring areas and on sites with the best facilities. One exception to this rule is the holiday-village-type site, where the proprietors may charge a low overnight fee in the hope of recouping their expenses by your patronage of their restaurants, shops, bingo halls and fruit machines. You'll find that some site owners charge a fixed fee for each outfit, while others charge on a 'per person per night' basis, but generally speaking a family of two adults and two children shouldn't have to pay very much for each night's stay on an average site.

Some sites offer reductions for weekly or fortnightly bookings, though there may not be a refund if you leave early. If you arrive at a site and are told that the minimum rate is so much for a week's stay, it is only fair to insist on having a quick look over the site first of all to make sure you are going to like it.

Pets on caravan sites

Children and dogs may be charged a lower rate than adults at some sites, while at others the fee may be the same – if they are allowed. I don't think I have ever come across a site that banned children but there are plenty – and some people may say rightly so – that ban dogs.

If you intend to take a dog with you, then it is essential to check in advance whether the sites you have chosen will accept and welcome it. If they do, then it is a matter of politeness to keep the animal under proper control, and this usually means keeping him tethered to the caravan on site and exercising him elsewhere. Take a dog away from his home environment and he is likely to act very differently from the way he does at home.

It is often kinder to take your dog with you than to leave it with friends or in a kennel, but remember that cats become more attached to places than to people and it can be very distressing for a cat to be taken away from the home environment.

Site guides

So much then for the types of site you are likely to find, but where are they? The answer is that they are all over the country, though obviously there are more in those areas popular with holidaymakers than elsewhere. To find out the exact locations you will have to acquire some sort of site guide. These are published by the clubs, by the motoring organizations, by the regional tourist boards and by general publishers – notably those associated with magazines on caravanning. The latter type are sold at most newsagents and booksellers during the spring and summer.

Most site guides will tell you not only where the sites are but how many caravans they will hold, what facilities you can expect to find, whether dogs are permitted, who the owner is and what his telephone number is; the Ordnance Survey map grid reference may also be given, and if so this is extremely valuable in locating the site and the best approach road. The favourite map used for site guide references has until recently been the 1-inch Ordnance Survey publication, but these maps are gradually being replaced by 1:50,000-scale metric maps. Since not all the country is at present covered by the 1:50,000 series (which are about $1\frac{1}{4}$ inches to the mile) check with your site guide index to see which maps are referred to.

The site guide will normally tell you whether you are expected to supply your own chemical toilet or whether flush toilets or chemical toilets are available on site. Opening dates will be quoted and in some cases it may say that advance booking is advised, essential or not accepted. Even if not essential, advance booking may be advisable if you are going to a popular spot in the height of summer. You can write a letter before leaving home or, if you are moving on from day to day, telephone the site the day before your arrival or even a few hours before, to save a wasted journey.

If you arrive at a site that apparently has room to spare, but the site warden tells you he is full, then take his word for it – though the site is not physically full up it probably contains as many vans as the number for which it is licensed, and you can't expect the site owner to jeopardize his licence just to squeeze you in. So if you are going to an area with few sites, make a reservation (if only by telephone) in advance. If you are going to an area with lots of sites, it is still wisest to arrive early so that you can move on if there is no room at your first choice.

At most sites you are expected to stop at the booking office, usually just inside the main gate, to get instructions on where to pitch; at others you may be expected to drive in and get your outfit pitched before anyone approaches you. There are no formalities and usually no forms to fill in at British sites, but you may be given, say, a sticker for your car windscreen so that you can gain re-admittance to the site. You may have to pay in advance or, occasionally, if you don't know how long you will be staying, you may pay when you leave.

CARAVAN AND CAMPING PARKS

NAME AND ADDRESS OF PARK
Position of park on national road system indicated thus (T1)

Amenities legend: Showers · Laundry Room · Public Telephone · Cafe/Restaurant Take Away Food · Shop · TV Room · Indoor Recreational Facilities · Outdoor Children's Play Centre · Field Game Activities · Gas Mantles on Sale on Site · No dogs allowed

Name and Address of Park	Telephone	PITCHES					AMENITIES	Duration of Season	OVERNIGHT		WEEKLY	
		Area in acres	No. of pitches	Number of Caravans to let on site	No. of pitches available for touring caravans	No. of pitches available for tents			£ Per Unit	£ Per Person	£ Per Unit	£ Per Person
CO. CAVAN												
SHERCOCK Lakelands Caravan Park (off T24 North of Shercock)	Shercock 60	3½	40	12	12	16	Showers, Laundry Room, Public Telephone, Cafe/Restaurant, Shop, Outdoor Play Centre, Gas	Easter to 31st Oct.	1.00	0.05	6.00	0.30
VIRGINIA Lough Ramor Caravan Park, Ryefield off Kells Road (T35) 3 miles south of Virginia.		1½	19	2	10	7	Showers, Outdoor Play Centre	All year round	0.50	0.05	3.00	0.30
CO. CLARE												
KILKEE Ryan's Caravan Park (T41)	Kilkee 82	9	110	70	10	10	Showers, Laundry Room, Public Telephone, TV Room, Indoor Recreational, Outdoor Play Centre, Gas	1 April–20 Sept.	1.00		7.00	
KILRUSH Aylevarroo Caravan Park T41 via Ennis, L51 via Tarbert-Kilimer Ferry, 2 miles from Kilrush	Kilrush 102, 199	6½	38	8	15	14	Showers, Laundry Room, Public Telephone, TV Room, Indoor Recreational, Outdoor Play Centre, Field Game Activities, No dogs allowed	Easter and From 31 May–7 Sept.	0.85		5.10	

Typical site guide entry

Sometimes there are daily deliveries of milk and newspapers to the site shop, and you can order these when you check in. If you are paying in advance, mention whether or not you will be using an awning with your van—sometimes there is an extra charge for these, for after all they take up a lot of additional space.

Selecting your pitch

Naturally you will want to find as level a pitch as possible for your van, though on most British sites there are no concrete 'hard-standings' for touring caravans. In most cases you will find yourself pitching the caravan somewhere in a grassy field, even if there are made-up roads to the individual plots.

Choose somewhere that isn't too uneven, for though the van is fitted with wind-down corner legs to help you set it level, you want to minimize your task—after all, you're on holiday! If the ground is soft, place something solid under the caravan feet (carry some flat pieces of wood in your car boot) to stop the legs sinking. Don't pitch your caravan in a hollow because if it rains during the night you may find yourself stepping out into puddles. Make sure you know where the toilet blocks are—not too far away if you think you might need them in the night—and also the fire extinguishers, site shop, etc.

On nearly all sites you will be able to leave your car parked alongside the caravan, so you will be able to leave the electric plug fitted if you want to power appliances in the van from the spare lead connected to the car battery. But don't reach the stage where the car battery will not start the car next morning. Some sites have car parks near the main entrance and often there is a stipulation that caravanners arriving back at site late at night must leave their cars in the late arrivals' car park until morning so that they don't disturb other residents.

If you are caravanning in the winter season, make particularly sure that you have easy access to your pitch by road, just in case the weather takes a turn for the worse and you want to move on. You will also want to set up your caravan nearer the amenities block, though of course this should be a lot easier out of season when the sites are less crowded.

If the approach to your pitch is downhill, remember you've got to get back up again when the time comes to leave, and that you may get less traction than you are used to if you have to cross wide expanses of wet grass. No doubt you would get a push, but it is better to avoid the embarrassment and hard work of a push by a little forethought.

Site manners

Always remember the golden rule that a caravan site should look as clean and tidy—cleaner and tidier if possible—when you leave as when you arrive. You will probably find litter bins and dustbins dotted around the site for your rubbish—so use them. If you can't find a bin, then keep your rubbish in a box or bucket inside the van till you find somewhere to deposit it.

Keep a proper waste bucket or container under the sink outlet and make sure you empty it at regular intervals into the right drain. And do bear in mind all the site rules about keeping the noise down, keeping animals under control and keeping fire extinguishers unobstructed.

Choosing continental sites

Continental sites are often graded by their national tourist boards, with the high-category sites having more facilities and correspondingly higher charges; there is no such official system in Britain, though some publications and organizations like to apply their own grading system. This is a very thorny subject, for while a site with every modern facility and convenience may warrant five stars in one person's book, the chap who wants a quiet field with nothing but a water tap might dismiss it out of hand. Those countries that award stars, rosettes or whatever to particular sites may do so for varying reasons, so check what their criteria are before aiming for the continental site with the most stars.

There are several good continental site guides available in Britain, some published here and some imported. Once again the motoring organizations and magazine publishers produce guides, but the most comprehensive are those published in the countries themselves. The best place to check for these is a good bookseller or map retailer, or you might enquire at the tourist office of the country concerned. Very often the tourist boards produce leaflets free of charge listing the biggest and most popular sites in particular areas.

Most continental sites are well equipped, and this is especially true of those in the tourist areas of France, Spain, Italy, Germany and other countries popular with tourists. Here site fees are much cheaper than hotel costs.

But whether you want continental sophistication or a rural retreat in an English field, caravanning can provide the answer.

Chapter 13
Going abroad

To have a caravan and not to venture across to the Continent is to miss half the fun. The idea of family camping really began just across the Channel, in France, and as soon as you drive out of the Channel port of your arrival you will notice a different attitude towards camping. And I use the word 'camping' on purpose — for on the Continent you'll find no distinction made between the trailer caravanner, the motor caravanner and the tent camper. Outside Britain, everyone who enjoys one of these pastimes is a camper and is welcome wherever the internationally used 'camping' sign is displayed.

Booking a ferry

Wherever you decide to go for your continental tour, you have unfortunately to cross a very expensive strip of water — the English Channel. For reasons that don't concern us here, the rates for ferrying vehicles to and fro across the Channel are high. Vehicle fares are worked out on the basis of length, so it is important for you to know the 'shipping length' of your caravan.

The shipping length is the overall length from the tip of the coupling to the farthest projection at the back end, and you will probably find it mentioned in the caravan brochure; if not, get out a tape measure. Unfortunately most caravan manufacturers seem to take little notice of the length classifications ferry companies use in their fare calculations and many produce vans that are only an inch or two outside cheaper fare structures. When you realize that this means a difference of several pounds on each return trip, you will see the importance of studying shipping lengths before buying your van if you intend to make regular sorties across to the Continent.

When you come to book the ferry crossing, you will find that the car and trailer are assessed independently, so you will pay one rate for the car and one for the caravan. In addition, of course, there will be the individual fares for each member of your party. You will find concessions on some ferry operators' routes (for instance, the car may travel free with four adult fare-paying passengers — though you will still have to pay the full rate for the van), while excess fares are charged for caravans on some other routes. Because they are over 6 feet high, caravans have to occupy commercial vehicle space in some ferries with low-roof car decks; on these routes there is usually a high-vehicle surcharge. The height of touring

The adventure of a continental holiday by caravan starts as soon as you drive on to one of today's modern cross-Channel car ferries

caravans also means that they cannot be taken on regular cross-Channel air ferry services.

Almost all modern Channel ferries are of the drive-on/drive-off type and you will be allowed to drive your outfit, coupled up, into the ship. Make sure the car and caravan handbrakes are firmly applied before you go upstairs to the passenger lounge, and also make sure all the gas equipment is turned off and the gas bottle turned off at the regulator.

If you read the terms of booking when you get your ferry tickets, you will notice that you are allowed to take up to three full cylinders of gas on board with you, but if you are carrying gas you are supposed to let the ferry company know this when you arrive at the port. In practice many people don't do this, but you should, just in case. In the unlikely event of there being a fire on board, it is essential for the crew to know if their ship is carrying bottles of highly inflammable gas and to know exactly where they are.

Your caravan and car should of course have been fitted with GB plates in preparation for the trip, but in case you remember only at the last moment, these (and other items such as breakdown kits, warning triangles and tow ropes) are usually available at the port from motoring organization offices or even from the ferry company. Nationality plates or stickers should be of the approved (black on white) type and attached to the nearside rear; they should be in an area that is illuminated at night. The yellow reflective GB plates that appeared and were the vogue a couple of years back, when reflective number plates made their début, are not legally recognized. I have never heard of anyone being stopped for having the wrong sort of GB plate – or indeed for not having one – but it is against the law, impolite and possibly dangerous not to have them fitted to both car and van.

If your outfit complies with the 50 mph towing limit regulations in Britain, you will of course have a '50' sticker on the back of your caravan too – though naturally this has no significance on the Continent. In fact it may cause confusion in some areas, where some official may think you are restricted to 50 *kilometres* an hour, so it is best to cover the '50' with tape or a stick-on GB plate. Don't forget to uncover it again when you arrive back this side of the Channel.

Speed limits

Speaking of speed limits, most countries, like Britain, have specific speed limits for cars drawing trailers and caravans. It is your responsibility to find out what the limit is in the country or countries you are about to visit

Continental road signs

The rule on the Continent is priority always to the right unless you are travelling on a priority road – which has the yellow diamond sign in advance of junctions

End of priority road

Minimum distance between vehicles

Road with motorway rules – only motor traffic, no stopping etc – but not built to motorway standard

New standard STOP sign being introduced in Europe

End of 'motorway type' restrictions on road – not built to motorway standards

and to make sure you stick to it. Naturally you should also be familiar with all the other non-towing regulations applicable; both major motoring organizations publish guides to motoring on the Continent.

Insurance

These days your car insurance policy must cover you for the most basic insurance risks demanded by those countries within the Common Market (France, Belgium, the Netherlands, Luxembourg, Italy, West Germany, Denmark and the Republic of Ireland), but these requirements are sometimes very basic indeed and may well not cover you when towing. It is still wisest to ask your insurance broker for the traditional green card insurance cover, and in doing so make it perfectly clear that you will be towing a trailer abroad; the green card will be specially endorsed to this effect. Don't forget also that the caravan policy must be altered if you want cover outside Britain. This will cost you a bit extra.

Other documents you will need are the car log book (a photostat copy will do), a letter authorizing you to drive if the car doesn't belong to you—if, for instance, it is a company car—and an international driving permit (IDP) or a translation of your licence if you are visiting certain countries. If you are going to Spain, you should also obtain a bail bond, which will stop the police impounding your outfit should you be unlucky enough to get involved in an accident. The bail bond and IDP are available from the AA or RAC.

Carnets

You will also hear campers and caravanners who visit the Continent talking about 'carnets'. There are two types: the camping carnet, which is reasonably important though not essential, and the customs carnet, which now is relatively unimportant. The camping carnet is a small card issued by camping and caravan clubs and by the motoring clubs affiliated to the international touring organizations. It carries your personal particulars and photograph, and is renewable over a period of three years. There are some continental sites (not a huge proportion) that will not admit you without such a card and there are also some that will give you a discount if you show it at the booking office.

But the main advantage of this carnet is that it is normally accepted in lieu of your passport when the site owner wants to record details of your name, home address, etc, for his police records. Every site operator has to make a note of who is staying at the site and this record is open to inspection by the police. Occasionally a site operator will ask you to lodge your carnet with him until you leave, as an additional precaution, and if you particularly like the site you have little to lose in the rare occurrence of his being dishonest.

If the site official wants you to leave your passport with him—don't. Passports are very valuable documents and are not the sort of thing to leave with strangers (strictly speaking 'your' passport does not belong to you anyway; it is the property of the Crown). By all means show the gentleman your passport, but leave him only your carnet if he insists on holding something. Sometimes if you agree to pay your site fees in advance he will relax his ideas on holding on to your documents—but then you have a problem if you decide you don't like the site and want to move on.

The other sort of carnet you may hear mentioned is the *carnet de passages en douane*, or customs carnet. This is a document that at one time had to be obtained before you could 'temporarily export' your caravan to another country and was a safeguard against the possibility of your selling it while abroad and contravening the country's tax laws. Nowadays you can forget about the customs carnet unless you are visiting very farflung areas—it has been abolished in Western Europe.

Planning ahead

It may sound silly to say that you should know where you are going when you leave for a continental holiday, but I mean you should have a sound route planned in advance. There is a good motorway network in most Western European countries—many of you will have driven solo cars abroad before anyway and will be familiar with them—and large distances can be covered, but it is best not to be too ambitious. Driving a solo car in Britain, you should aim to cover no more than 300 miles in a day; driving a car plus caravan in a strange country, you should have a target distance of far less than this.

Whether it's you or some other member of the family, the driver is on holiday too and he doesn't want to arrive at the caravan site too tired to enjoy anything but a good night's sleep. Caravanning requires an added amount of concentration on the road too, so make sure you stop every couple of hours on a long journey to stretch your legs and have a refreshing non-alcoholic drink.

When driving on the Continent, look out for the internationally known 'camping' sign

Continental sites

Most continental countries seem to take leisure pursuits rather more seriously than we do and you will find many European caravan and camping sites equipped with every facility you could wish for – including games rooms, swimming pools, shops and restaurants. Naturally they tend to be very popular and a question that's often asked is whether there is any necessity to book your pitch in advance. The answer depends largely on where you are going. If you are heading for the South of France, the Costa Brava or any popular holiday areas, and you want to guarantee a pitch right on the beach, then yes, book ahead – if you can. Foreign site operators are notoriously bad at replying to letters from prospective visitors.

If you are prepared to take a pitch at a site a few miles inland (where the charges may be considerably less, the facilities less overworked and pitching a good deal easier), then in most areas there should be no need to book in advance.

Once you decide you like a particular area and would like to stay there the night, or for a few days, the rule is the same as when touring a popular area of Britain – start looking for a site early. Just after lunch is a good time, because many people will have moved on after breakfast but you'll be getting in before the late afternoon rush.

Many continental sites offer mains electricity hook-ups, but don't take all your electrical appliances from home in the belief that such hook-ups are a general feature. If you intend to make use of mains electricity supply, make sure you take with you a suitable length of proper outdoor cable and that any connections made at the van have weatherproof plugs and sockets. For the connection at the other end of the cable you will almost certainly have to buy a local plug, as the pattern varies a lot from place to place.

When to travel

Don't forget to consider climate when you plan your holiday abroad. Baking hot climates may be all very well when you are jetted to your hotel and waited on hand and foot when you get there; you may prefer something a little more temperate when you have first to drive there and then to cater for yourself.

If you have children you may be committed to taking your main summer holiday in July or August and at that time temperatures will be at their highest in southern Europe. So if you don't like things too hot, you should avoid southern France, Spain, Italy, Greece and the other Mediterranean lands. Remember, too, that foreign families also have schoolchildren, so sites will be most crowded in these areas at these times.

Health problems

Don't neglect medical insurance – doctors' fees can be sky-high abroad. British nationals in PAYE employment are now eligible for the same national health benefits as residents when visiting EEC countries, but you must contact your Department of Health and Social Security local office before leaving home in order to obtain the necessary claim forms, and in any case it's usually a case of paying the fee at the time and claiming your money back later. Private health insurance schemes – some policies also cover you for loss of vehicle and breakdown insurance – are offered by some insurance companies, by the motoring organizations and by camping and caravan clubs. For peace of mind if nothing else they are worthwhile.

Preparing the outfit

Your car and caravan should be thoroughly roadworthy before leaving home and you should carry with you adequate supplies of things that are likely to break or get lost – spare bulbs, fanbelt, contact set, radiator hose, spark plugs, etc.

If you don't have one already, make sure you fit a good, wide-view towing mirror to the nearside of your car (remember it will be the offside in Europe) and get a set of lens convertors to make your headlamps dip to the right. The lens covers should be yellow if you will be driving through France at night.

A final word

You will get used to driving on the 'wrong' side of the road very quickly, but one word of warning: if you stop your caravan in a roadside lay-by for a short break, remember that the caravan door now opens out on to the road, not the grass verge — and watch out for boisterous children who might jump out into the road instead of the pathway.

Chapter 14
Useful information

Clubs to join

Camping Club of Great Britain & Northern Ireland
(open to tent campers, trailer and motor caravanners; caravanners have their own section—the British Caravanners' Club)
Address: 11 Lower Grosvenor Place, London SW1W OEY

01 828 1012

Auto Camping Club
(open to tent campers, trailer and motor caravanners)
Address: 5 Dunsfold Rise, Coulsdon, Surrey CR3 2ED

01 660 8656

Caravan Club
(Open to trailer and motor caravanners)
Address: 65 South Molton Street, London W1Y 2AB

01 629 6441

Trailer Caravan Club
(open to trailer and motor caravanners)
Address: 29 Stoneycroft, Warners End, Hemel Hempstead, Hertfordshire

0442 51294

Before you hire a caravan . . .

Is your car fitted with a towing bracket, 50-millimetre towing ball and seven-pin electric socket?
Do you need additional rear-view mirrors?
Is the car in sound mechanical condition?
Have you told your car insurance company?
Is the caravan fully insured?
What equipment is supplied with the van?
Have you checked the inventory?
Have you made up a rear number plate for the van?
Is the caravan the right size and weight for your car and your family?

Which tyre combinations are legal?

Tow car front	Tow car rear	Caravan	
Cross-ply	Cross-ply	Cross-ply	√
Radial	Cross-ply	Cross-ply	×
Radial	Radial	Cross-ply	√
Radial	Radial	Radial	√
Cross-ply	Radial	Cross-ply	√
Cross-ply	Cross-ply	Radial	√
Cross-ply	Radial	Radial	√

Legal requirements for towing at 50 mph

Private motor cars may tow braked trailer caravans with a single axle or close-coupled twin axles at up to 50 mph on British roads not carrying a lower limit, *provided*

1. The maximum gross weight of the caravan does not exceed the kerbside weight of the car
2. The maximum gross weight of the caravan is marked conspicuously on its near or left-hand side
3. The kerbside weight of the car is marked conspicuously inside or on its near or left-hand side
4. Both weights are in the same units, which must be kilograms if expressed in metric measure
5. The caravan carries a '50' sign of the approved colour and dimensions at the rear

Six points that make a good tow car

Strong rear suspension
High weight
Short tail overhang
High engine torque at low revs
Strong clutch
Well-spaced gear ratios

Financing your caravan purchase

Overdraft – a low rate of interest, but you must have something the bank can hold as security (e.g. stocks and shares)
Insurance – if you have an endowment policy you may be able to borrow from the insurance company
Personal bank loan – a flat rate of interest over the whole term; more expensive than an overdraft but easier to obtain
Finance house personal loan – similar to personal bank loan, though interest rates are usually higher
Credit card – if you have a high enough credit limit. Interest rate is fixed and you can choose your own repayment period (within limits)
Second mortgage – interest rates usually very high – and at worst you could be putting your house at risk
Hire purchase – high interest rates, and until you have paid off one-third of the loan the finance company can repossess the goods if you default

Don't forget...

- ✓ crockery
- ✓ cutlery
- ✓ tea pot/coffee pot ✗
- ✓ salt and pepper
- ✓ tin opener
- ✓ bottle opener/corkscrew
- ✓ frying pan
- ✓ saucepans
- kettle
- food containers
- washbowl
- radio
- ✓ site guides and maps
- ✓ sleeping bags
- pillows
- blankets ✗
- ✓ towels
- ✓ tea towels
- ✓ toilet paper
- ✓ coathangers
- first aid kit
- personal washing materials
- matches ✗
- ✓ waste-water bucket
- litter bin
- washing-up liquid
- ✓ corner leg brace

- ✓ step
- ✓ awning
- ✓ water carriers
- toilet tent
- ✓ chemical toilet ✗
- ✓ toilet fluid/powder
- ✓ gas
- ✓ regulator and spanner
- clothes
- boots and shoes
- ✓ outdoor furniture
- fire extinguisher
- ✓ toolkit
- spare keys
- pens and pencils
- camera
- coolbox
- egg cups
- gas mantles
- fluorescent tubes
- kitchen roll
- money
- credit cards
- tissues
- swimwear
- torch

(handwritten) BELTS
(handwritten) PANS FRUIT-TOPS

Choosing a caravan site

Check:
ease of access

position(s) of toilets, washing facilities, water collection
   and disposal points

overnight and weekly fees

whether dogs are permitted

availability of food, gas, accessories,

other facilities

nearness to busy roads/railway lines

flat or undulating ground

whether pitches are numbered or random

local attractions (something to do in wet weather)

restrictions on late arrivals, use of radios, etc

(handwritten notes)
MARMALADE
PRESSURE COOKER
BREAD KNIFE.
BOOKS
SLIPPERS ✗
WINE & BEER
RAZORS
CASSETTES
OXTER SPRAY
JUMP LEADS ✓
EXTENSION LEADS ✓
SNORKEL ✓
WETSUIT
SPARE BATTERY ✓
INDIGESTION TABLETS

(handwritten second column)
WASH CARAVAN
REMOVE BATTERY
SWITCH OFF WATER
BINOCULARS
ICE CUBES
BAR B Q
CHARCOAL
— SHINKWRAP

Foreign travel—
extra equipment

camping carnet
continental site guide
conversion tables
GB plates
foreign touring insurance
green card insurance
car log book
letter of authority (if car isn't yours)
passports
phrase book(s)
vaccination certificates
travel sickness tablets
water purification tablets
currency/travel cheques
extra food
Some countries
international driving permit—IDP
bail bond (Spain only)
visas
warning triangles

First aid equipment

rolled bandages
triangular bandages
cotton wool
lint
plasters
sterile dressings
eye bath
safety pins
scissors (round ends)
aspirins
travel sickness tablets
insect repellent
skin-burn cream
tweezers
petroleum jelly
water purification tablets
first aid instruction book

Calculating your weight allowance

CARAVAN maximum gross weight	A
CARAVAN ex-works weight	B
TOW CAR kerbside weight	C

Write in the weights for your car and the caravan you have or are considering buying. Subtracting B from A will give you your weight allowance for personal gear—you will need a minimum of 3 hundredweight for a family of four. If C is greater than A, you will be able to tow at 50 mph on British roads without a lower limit, provided your car and caravan are suitably marked; see page 49.

Acknowledgements

The author and publisher thank the following for permission to reproduce the photographs listed below:

Pages 10, 48, 76 (below), the Caravan Club; pages 13 and 24, CI Caravans; pages 47 and 72, Peter Baker; page 15, Thomson T-Line Caravans; page 54, Blacks of Greenock; page 76 (above) Safari (Water Treatments) Ltd; page 79, Feature Photos; page 84, British Railways Board; page 47 (left), Nu-Swift, page 39 (left), Barnett Plastics Ltd; pages 59–60, Jupiter Pump Co Ltd; page 89, Astral; page 87, Eccles (Adrian Flowers); pages 7, 53, 55, 56, 57, 58, 61, Vernons.

Index